Dear Jorge,

Whose many splendid
strengths are admirable
and appreciated.

Saludos,

Robert Kaplan

Fear
Your Strengths

What You Are Best at
Could Be Your Biggest Problem

Robert E. Kaplan
Robert B. Kaiser

BK

Berrett–Koehler Publishers, Inc.
San Francisco
a BK Business book

Berrett-Koehler Publishers, Inc.
235 Montgomery Street, Suite 650
San Francisco, CA 94104-2916
Tel: (415) 288-0260 Fax: (415) 362-2512 www.bkconnection.com

Ordering Information

Quantity sales. Special discounts are available on quantity purchases by corporations, associations, and others. For details, contact the "Special Sales Department" at the Berrett-Koehler address above.

Individual sales. Berrett-Koehler publications are available through most bookstores. They can also be ordered directly from Berrett-Koehler: Tel: (800) 929-2929; Fax: (802) 864-7626; www.bkconnection.com

Orders for college textbook/course adoption use. Please contact Berrett-Koehler: Tel: (800) 929-2929; Fax: (802) 864-7626.

Orders by U.S. trade bookstores and wholesalers. Please contact Ingram Publisher Services, Tel: (800) 509-4887; Fax: (800) 838-1149; E-mail: customer. service@ingrampublisherservices.com; or visit www.ingrampublisherservices .com/Ordering for details about electronic ordering.

Berrett-Koehler and the BK logo are registered trademarks of Berrett-Koehler Publishers, Inc.

Printed in the United States of America

Berrett-Koehler books are printed on long-lasting acid-free paper. When it is available, we choose paper that has been manufactured by environmentally responsible processes. These may include using trees grown in sustainable forests, incorporating recycled paper, minimizing chlorine in bleaching, or recycling the energy produced at the paper mill.

Library of Congress Cataloging-in-Publication Data

Kaplan, Robert E.
    Fear your strengths : what you are best at could be your biggest problem /
    Robert E. Kaplan and Robert B. Kaiser. -- 1st ed.
        p. cm.
    Includes bibliographical references and index.
    ISBN 978-1-60994-904-4 (hardcover)
    1. Leadership. 2. Leadership--Psychological aspects. 3. Executive ability.
    I. Kaiser, Robert B. II. Title.
    HD57.7.K365 2013
    658.4'092--dc23
                                                            2012044412

First Edition

18 17 16 15 14 13   10 9 8 7 6 5 4 3 2 1

Interior design and project management: Dovetail Publishing Services
Cover design and production: Nancy Austin

Contents

Introduction

THIS BOOK IS THE CULMINATION of the surprising epiphanies and serendipitous insights we have garnered over a lifetime of working with senior leaders, including the CEOs of major corporations, to help them increase their effectiveness. We did not set out to discover what the leadership field has overlooked, but over the years, as we helped these leaders look in the mirror, each little revelation was like a curtain lifting on a neglected part of the drama of leadership. Most of what we have observed is in plain view yet its significance has been missed or it hasn't been put into practice.

Fifteen years ago, a routine executive assessment provided us with just such a seminal moment. We were working with an executive whose 360-degree evaluation characterized him, as one coworker had put it, as "an elemental force in nature." Yet his effectiveness as a leader was less than optimal. "Look," we offered, "you are clearly a force to be reckoned with." Then we took it a step further. "The problem is that at times you're *overly* forceful." There it was. In a way we had never quite realized or articulated before, we acknowledged that too much strength can be a weakness. It dawned on us that doing too much of something was as much of a problem as doing too little of it.

Put differently, your strengths can work against you. Many leaders know this on some intuitive level, but they tend not to accept it in practice. It's not even in most managers' vocabulary. Mainly, they think of leadership development as working on their weaknesses. No wonder. The tools used to assess managers are not equipped to pick up on strengths overplayed. In performance appraisals, managers are typically rated as not meeting expectations, meeting expectations, or exceeding expectations. In coworker feedback questionnaires, popularly known as 360s, managers are typically rated as ineffective, effective, or very effective. Nowhere in most assessments is there language or diagnostics that can reveal when someone is overdoing it—when more is *not* better.

The lack of attention paid to strengths overplayed has persisted despite the glut of books—most notably, Marcus Buckingham and Donald Clifton's *Now, Discover Your Strengths*—exhorting managers to focus

2

on their strengths. Remarkably, in their enthusiasm to accentuate the positive, Buckingham and other strengths advocates fail to point out to their managerial audience the ever-present danger of taking their strengths too far.

In our consulting work, we have increasingly focused on making leaders aware of that danger and enabling the important developmental work necessary to mitigate it. We have enjoyed enviable firsthand exposure to senior leaders, conducted thousands of assessments of individual executives, and collected reams of data. We have put our thinking into practice in the form of an assessment tool, the Leadership Versatility Index (LVI, US Patent No. 7,121,830), a coworker-feedback questionnaire (360) that we designed expressly to assess for strengths overplayed. It has in turn served to further refine our thinking.

Our statistical findings as well as our practical experience form the basis of this book. We regularly illustrate our insights with case studies of executives with whom we have worked closely and extensively. To guard the executives' anonymity, the protagonist of each "case" is actually a composite and real names are not used. But the anecdotes, experiences, and voices we describe are unfailingly real, as are the problems we identified and the solutions that were implemented.

Among our most surprising findings has been that leaders often have a hard time acknowledging their strengths in the first place. Once, when preparing for a feedback session, we were startled to see that the executive was so highly rated that there seemed to be practically nothing wrong with his leadership. "We've got nothing to work with," we thought. It was unnerving. It turned out, however, that there was plenty of "ammunition" in the positive feedback. This individual underestimated his assets and, as a result, sometimes overcompensated, making him less effective than he might have been.

Gifted leaders, we have found, are often the last ones to acknowledge their gifts, even when they have ample evidence and feedback that attests to it. The practical fact is that the only way to manage your strengths is to accept them. If you literally don't know your own strength, you have no way to calibrate or modulate it. In a relentless effort to be better, you have no way of knowing if you are going too far. One of the main missions of this book is to help you come to grips with your strengths and make full use of them without overdoing it.

We have also found that, for most executives, waking up to the potential dangers inherent in their strengths can be a vertigo-inducing shock. As one senior leader admitted, "The idea is unsettling. It's chilling. I really mean that." When leaders are faced with the prospect that the very intensity that fueled their rise to the top can be smothering their coworkers and sabotaging their effectiveness, they are often panic-stricken at the thought of needing to ease up. "I'm afraid I'll lose my edge," is what we often hear, a reaction that is natural but misguided. In what may be the cruelest of ironies, overplayed strengths are often at the root of career failure. Analyses of derailed leaders time and again point to the excessive reliance on qualities that were key to past success but less relevant to the current role. We have learned that to stop overplaying a strength does not mean, as many leaders fear, to stop using it. It means using the strength more selectively. As another hyperintense executive finally realized, "I don't have to give up my fast ball. I just don't have to throw it all the time."

Coming to grips with the need to modulate your strengths is some of the hardest developmental work you will ever do. After all, it's your strengths that have made you successful. Why would you ever tamper with a winning formula? As one client quipped, "Overplaying your strengths: that's a comfy, cozy place to be." We wrote this book to ease the transition, to offer you real developmental leverage on both a behavioral level and a personal level. The work on yourself isn't therapy. It is a plainspoken and useful approach that helps you trace your leadership behavior back to the "crooked thinking" and "trigger points" that can throw it off kilter. We offer a practical psychology of leadership—a better way for leaders to get a reading on their performance, one that is truer to the realities of managerial work. Leadership development amounts to moving an individual from point A to point B. Each of the insights and practices described in this book offers the leader added leverage for making that move.

Chapter 1

Strengths Beget Weaknesses— In Two Very Different Ways

RICH SPIRE'S TALENT SHIMMERS. He embodies everything that the word "leader" has come to mean in the business world. The same raw, competitive instinct he had as a baseball player in Little League and right through college—always swinging for the fences—animates his leadership today. As president of a sector of a large, fast-growing technology company, he never shies away from making big, bold moves. He knows his business and is uncannily adept at identifying industry trends and opportunities. He has a positive attitude that won't quit. "Self-actualization," he often says, "comes from the impossible dream achieved."

Spire is a commanding presence with a true gift for articulating his vision in a way that persuades and excites people—not just in broad terms but, as one colleague says, "with enough color and granularity that people can grasp their portion of the vision."

"He has more potential than anyone I know," says another. "He has huge talent, intelligence, and strategic insight. And it's all wrapped up in a charismatic package."

What could possibly be wrong with this picture?

As is often the case with natural leaders, the use of power comes easily to Spire, but perhaps too easily. He so stunningly wields his intellectual firepower and charisma that he makes it a daunting task for others to contend with him. His forceful leadership—a good thing when used in correct proportion—effectively renders him unable to elicit, nurture, and benefit from other input in the organization. "I think he stakes out his positions too early," says one colleague. "People then seek to be in agreement with him rather than bringing their best thinking."

What's more, Spire's penchant for bold, strategic action often exceeds his organization's ability to keep up. It isn't just that he is too aggressive strategically; he correspondingly neglects—and even undervalues—the operational component of his strategy. His CFO puts it this way: "[Spire's] vision outstripped our internal capacity. His strategic reach was too great to be executed with the bench strength we had. It's useful to have vision, but he needs to implement it in a more measured way."

8

Facing into the headwind of Spire's forceful personality and his voracious appetite to have a big impact, some people on his team simply give up trying to influence him. "It takes too much emotional energy to keep confronting this guy," says one, "and he isn't going to listen anyway." In defeating his loyal opposition, Spire puts himself and his organization at risk.

By taking his talents to such an extreme, Spire undermines those very talents. They in fact become a weakness. There is a tragic irony in this. What could be a great asset turns into, at least in part, a liability. It's an unfortunate loss for the leader and for his organization. Just like a point guard whose uncanny court vision causes him to make lightning-quick passes that catch his teammates flat-footed, or like a running back who is so fast he crashes into his own lineman, a leader of prodigious but immoderate talents will leave half of his team in the dust. A gift can often work against the gifted.

All managers, regardless of level, are likely to overuse their strengths. A leader's desire to be forceful and straightforward with direct reports becomes a tendency to be abusive and peremptory. A devotion to consensus-seeking breeds chronic indecision. An emphasis on being respectful of others degenerates into ineffectual niceness. The desire to turn a profit and serve shareholders becomes a preoccupation with short-term thinking. To the leader whose best tool is a hammer, everything is a nail. A leader who goes to his best tool in every situation, who consistently overplays his hand, may perform adequately, or even well, but he is ultimately far less effective than he might be. As one manager said about himself, "Overusing a strength is underperformance."

The irony that maximizing a strength corrupts it is beautifully captured in Sherwood Anderson's novel *Winesburg, Ohio*. An old writer on his death bed muses: "In the beginning when the world was young there were truths and they were beautiful, and then people came along. The moment a person took a truth to himself, called it his truth, and tried to live by it, he became grotesque, and the truth became a falsehood."

Overusing one's strength not only corrupts the strength, but it begets weakness in yet another way. What deforms leaders, makes them grotesque, is that not only do they embrace their strength as the only truth but they consequently ignore an equal and opposing strength. The result of this collateral damage is lopsided leadership: too much of one thing made worse by too little of its complement. When Rich Spire overplayed his considerable powers of persuasion, they drowned out his ability to hear the voices of his staff.

Likewise, Spire had the setting on his strategic ambition cranked up so high that it swamped its opposite, operational realism. His CFO, familiar with Rich's instinct to grab strategic ground, would often counsel him: "Let's make sure we execute in a measured way so growth won't just be a flash of light and burn out." Spire confessed, "I jump in with both hands and both feet because I only have one speed: high." For leaders like Spire, the challenge is to turn down the volume on his natural strength and turn it up on its opposite, which he usually ignores. It's all about getting the setting right on both dials.

This is a practical notion that goes back at least as far as Aristotle, who postulated that what is good, virtuous, and effective in thought and action is the midpoint between deficiency and excess. Aristotle's precept has often been mistaken to advocate moderation in all things. On the contrary, speaking of courage, or of compassion, he emphasized that what is needed is the right amount for the circumstances. "Anybody can become angry or give money, but to be angry with or to give money to the right person, and in the right amount, and at the right time, and for the right purpose, and in the right way—this is not within everybody's power and is not easy." There is no fixed setting on the dial for the proper use of a strength, a virtue. The volume needs to go up or down according to what the situation requires.

There is no better—or more extreme—case of corrupted strengths than that of Jeffrey Skilling, who as company president personified the infamous scandal at Enron. Although Rich Spire's voracious appetite for taking strategic ground crossed the line that separates productive from counterproductive, Skilling's unchecked growth mania eventually crossed the line from counterproductive to ruinous, unethical, and illegal. Skilling had a huge hand in Enron's collapse, which led to what was then, in 2001, history's largest corporate bankruptcy. At the time of this writing, he is in prison, several years into a 25-year sentence for conspiracy, fraud, and insider trading.

Jeffrey Skilling was brought to Enron to head its trading operation, a sideline business in what was primarily an old-line natural-gas company. Brilliant and creative, he saw and seized the opportunity to convert Enron's contracts to buy and sell natural gas into financial instruments that could be traded, something that had never been done in the industry. That was Skilling's strength: he was clever and visionary. But he overplayed that strength and took his business-building zeal beyond ethical limits. He used mark-to-market accounting to book the total estimated value of, say, a ten-year contract on the very day the contract was signed. He engineered financial deals, schemes really, that removed debt from Enron's balance sheet and thereby projected a false picture of the company's financial condition. In the end, Enron had borrowed $38 billion of which only $13 billion appeared on the balance sheet.

Skilling's leadership was lopsided in so many ways. A big-idea guy, he ignored the blocking and tackling of implementation. When picking people, he overvalued intellect and undervalued social skills. When rewarding people, he overrelied on money as a motivator but was personally abusive and grossly neglected the organization's increasingly destructive and corrupt culture.

Skilling was also a classic victim of the Peter Principle. He was made president of Enron despite coming from a consultant background devoid of operational experience on the industrial side. He lacked the practical experience to know there are some things you can't do. To compound the problem, Skilling either ignored or steamrolled Enron's Risk Assessment and Control (RAC) group, whose job it was to veto deals that broke the rules or ran exceedingly high business risks.

In the end, no one individual, discrete event, or single policy brought Enron down. The collapse was aided and abetted by CEO Kenneth Lay, CFO Andrew Fastow, and a host of other lieutenants, as well as the outside accounting firm, Arthur Anderson, which ultimately signed off on Enron's false financial statements. The book that chronicled Enron's downfall, *The Smartest Guys in the Room*, described it this way: "The scandal grew out of a steady accumulation of habits, values, and actions that began years before and finally spiraled out of control." But Skilling was the leader. Ultimately, it was his excessiveness and his lopsidedness that bred and sanctioned Enron's out-of-control culture.

The destructiveness of overweening strength can be seen in endless leadership examples, from the historically notorious, such as Hitler or Mao Zedong, to the ignominious, such as Jeffrey Skilling, to the immoderate, such as Rich Spire—each larger than life in his own context. However, there are also multitudes of leaders at all levels of every imaginable type of organization laboring in relative obscurity whose leadership is marred by the same fundamental dynamic. Daily organizational life is replete with examples, and the warning signs can be quite commonplace.

A most ordinary example is overtalking. Some leaders who excel at expressing themselves articulately and at great length have a lot to offer but don't know when to stop. Eventually, the energy goes out of the room. Other leaders who talk too much are storehouses of knowledge or great storytellers. They have the ability to hold the floor and they enjoy doing so immensely, but they ultimately lose their audience. That is because overtalkers of all stripes have one fatal flaw in common: they act as if there is nothing to be gained from hearing from others. The dial is cranked up too high on their strength—the ability to be articulate—and it's stuck at that setting, effectively precluding any ability to listen.

In one study we found that leaders are five times more likely to overdo a strength than their other attributes. Whatever they were best at, they got carried away with. Likewise, they tended to neglect the opposing and complementary behaviors. For instance, managers who, using the Gallup Strengths Finder instrument, categorized themselves as "Achiever," "Activator," and "Command" tended to be rated by coworkers as too forceful and not empowering or participative enough. Conversely, as you would expect, those classifying themselves as "Developer," "Harmony, and "Includer" were rated the opposite by coworkers. Don't just discover your strengths, as Gallup recommends; also understand how you use them, including what happens when you overuse them.

The signs and symptoms of overplayed strength are everywhere and affect every leader. It's not just that performance suffers; promising careers derail. Yet overuse of strengths is often overlooked because neither leaders nor their handlers are attuned to how strength can beget weakness. To be sure, not every weakness is a by-product of overused strength. Sometimes, it is a shortcoming that can be rectified by getting more experience or training or giving greater effort. But in every leader, in every person, there is at least one strong tendency that carries with it the risk of being *too* strong as well as a secondary risk of rendering the opposing tendency too weak. When this insidious lopsidedness takes hold in a leader—often very early in life—it can become chronic, deeply habitual, and in the worst cases virulent.

To paraphrase Ralph Waldo Emerson: you must stand in terror of your strengths.

Chapter 2

The Yin-Yang Responsibilities of a Leader

THERE IS NO BETTER single expression of ideal leadership than the ancient Chinese concept of yin and yang. The Chinese saw nature as the interplay of dualities that had both complementary and opposing characteristics—sky and earth, day and night, water and fire, active and passive, male and female. Neither element in the pair takes prominence or precedence, but each is useful and valid and reinforces the other in a positive dynamic. The familiar yin-yang symbol represents this perfectly, showing two black-and-white teardrop shapes, curled and flowing into each other, continually adapting to each other to form a continuous and complete circle. The elements are negative images of each other, yet they are interdependent and inextricable.

When it comes to leadership, the importance of this idea is a practical, not a philosophical, matter. Leaders are no strangers to the idea that skill sets come in pairs. They often refer to themselves as "balanced" or not, as "task-oriented" or "people-oriented." Despite this awareness, however, few leaders are able to combine opposite approaches in a holistic way. They usually resolve the tension between the two sides simply by taking a position and favoring one over the other. In fact, lopsided leadership could be described as dysfunctional duality, in which one element of a pair of strengths has grown to dominate and to stunt the other.

Some of this is the result of conscious decisions leaders make on a day-to-day basis, but much of it is tacit and unconscious, the product of leaders' innate qualities and experiences. All their lives they have learned to define their leadership persona on the basis of being one thing and not the other: If I am bold, I can never retreat. If I am a visionary, it is small-minded to worry about operational details. Over the course of a career, one strength hypertrophies while the other atrophies.

In the course of our work, we have concluded that there are two core dualities that confront all leaders: the need to be *forceful* combined with the need to be *enabling*, and the need to have a *strategic* focus combined with the need to have an *operational* focus.

Together these dualities constitute the "how" and the "what" of leading (see the figure). In the simplest terms, forceful leadership is taking the lead, and enabling leadership is making it possible for others to lead. The dynamic tension between the two sides determines *how* people work together. Strategic leadership is looking ahead and positioning the organization for the future, and operational leadership is about getting results in the short term. That dynamic tension determines *what* organizational issues managers focus on.

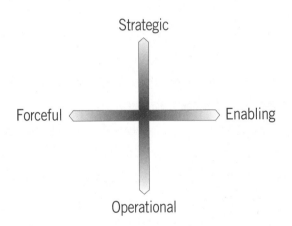

In our work with senior managers, we find lopsidedness over and over again, and nowhere is it plainer than in the statistical relationship between forceful leadership and enabling leadership. Roughly 7,000 managers ranging from mid-level to CEO have been rated by roughly 60,000 coworkers using our proprietary assessment tool called the Leadership Versatility

Index, and the findings have consistently shown a strong negative correlation. That is, the more forceful a leader, the less enabling that individual is likely to be. Conversely, the more enabling a leader is, the less forceful he or she is likely to be. In another study, we found that when managers were rated as doing "too much" of either forceful or enabling behavior, there was a 90 percent chance that they were also rated as doing "too little" of the other behavior.

Although most leaders overplay either the forceful or the enabling side of their repertoire, we have occasionally encountered a breed of executive who is deficient in both. One executive we knew had an outwardly strong personality—a resonant voice, a firm handshake, a confident air—but was strangely marginal in his own team meetings. In fact, someone unfamiliar with the situation would not have been able to tell that he was the team leader. This kind of "laissez faire" manager is essentially passive and disengaged and, not surprisingly, has been consistently rated by coworkers as even less effective than lopsided leaders.

Strategic leadership and operational leadership are also inversely related. There the negative correlation is dampened a bit by the low incidence of leaders who are rated as too strategic—indeed, most leaders aren't strategic enough. Nonetheless, when managers were rated as doing "too much" of either strategic or operational leadership, there was about an 80 percent chance that they were also rated as doing "too little" of the other behavior. The reality is that big-picture, visionary types tend not to be good at implementation, and the masters of implementation tend to ignore or underplay strategy.

The overall pattern could hardly be clearer. Lopsided leaders are the rule and not the exception.

Forceful and Enabling Leadership

Consider Carla Middleton. Born into difficult circumstances, she overcame them with a vengeance to become the first woman president at a prestigious liberal arts college. Throughout her career, her nagging sense of being "one-down" fueled her rapid ascent but also left an indelible imprint on her leadership style. This was a forceful leader who fed off her own intellect and energy and fairly reveled in her efficacy, so much so that she was quite poor at tapping into and encouraging the intellect and energy of other people.

Within a few months of taking her post, Carla had successfully launched an ambitious three-year capital campaign and, with the resulting funds, presided over the remaking of the school's physical plant—an undeniable success. Nevertheless, although faculty members grudgingly acknowledged her impressive achievements, they resented her centrist, noncollegial approach. Having won many admirers but few friends, she put herself in jeopardy. As one put it, "If she's got to be the star, fine, but if that star falls don't expect me to help out or care." Her approach also bred resentment among other members of the school's administration and greatly compromised her effectiveness. "If she wants to dictate the solution, I'll play along but not wholeheartedly," said a colleague.

In stark contrast, Billy Peoples was a great believer in enabling other people's talents. He spoke reverentially about the value that other people bring. He was a great listener and excelled at making decisions by consensus. One staff member observed admiringly: "Billy doesn't figure out solutions by himself; he gets others to collectively figure out what should be done." He was universally viewed as people-oriented and appreciated for it. He always treated other people with respect. In performance reviews he never tore away at the other person's self-esteem. His devotion to the team concept had roots deep in his upbringing. His parents raised him to be a high achiever and, just as important, to be a quintessential team player—humble, helpful, and fair-minded.

Unfortunately, Peoples did such a good job of giving other people a voice in decision making that his own voice was lost. Others often wondered where he stood. They wanted him to declare himself earlier and more forcefully, but his overdeveloped sense of humility held him back. His sincere but overplayed concern for others prevented him from making tough personnel decisions, and his boss often took him to task for that, telling him, "You're tolerant of people who just don't cut it, and you choose to live with situations that aren't working."

Though philosophical opposites, Carla Middleton and Billy Peoples took different roads to the same fate. Both tarnished their considerable strengths by taking them too far. Both were limited by one-sided notions of leadership rooted in their earlier experience. Ultimately, their lopsidedness jeopardized their organizations' goals and their own careers.

"Forceful" and "enabling" constitute broad classes of leadership behavior. Contained with each of them, however, are specific pairs of smaller-scope behaviors: to take charge and to empower, to declare and to listen, and to push for performance and to support. Each of those behaviors can be either virtues or, if taken to extremes, vices:

Table 2.1 Virtues and Vices of Forceful and Enabling Leadership

Forceful		Enabling	
Vices	Virtues	Virtues	Vices
Overcontrolling	Takes charge	Empowers	Trusts, doesn't verify
Dominates meetings	Declares	Listens	Receptive to a fault
Too demanding	Pushes	Supports	Too nice

Any given manager's aptitude will likely vary even among related behaviors. A forceful manager, for instance, may be quite adept at taking charge, but fall short in pushing for accountability. An enabling manager may be a good listener but struggle with delegating responsibility. What is lacking in most leaders is a fine-tuned sensibility to all behaviors on both sides of the ledger.

The relative importance of forceful and enabling leadership has been the subject of much debate over the years. In the 1960 classic *The Human Side of Enterprise*, Douglas McGregor made the case for enabling leaders. He argued that too many leaders subscribe to what he called Theory X, the belief that the average person doesn't like to work, avoids responsibility, and therefore must be forcefully managed. He pointed out that Theory X is a self-fulfilling prophecy: by assuming that employees have little drive and need constant supervision, you create a work environment of low expectations and low satisfaction in which there is little reason to take initiative. McGregor's Theory Y offered an alternate assumption that people are perfectly willing to work hard and take responsibility when given the chance. By doing so, he reasoned, you replace the vicious cycle of Theory X with a virtuous and far more productive one.

Abraham Zaleznik made largely the opposite, but equally compelling, case in 1989's *The Managerial*

Mystique: Restoring Leadership in Business. He argued that forceful, take-charge leadership is crucial to organizational effectiveness, and that its importance had been unfairly derided and diminished by the empowerment movement.

McGregor and Zaleznik each represent significant schools of thought in the leadership culture wars, and each camp tends to discredit and be dismissive of the other. In our work, it has not been hard to find outspoken advocates on either side. One senior manager, whose company had championed quality for ten years with considerable success, nevertheless expressed grave concern about its muffling effects: "When you focus so much on process, you tend to forget the role of personality and leadership."

An executive at a different organization held a similar view. "This corporation is full of round-worded, nice people who don't make a change," he said. "A whiff of brutal clarity, if it's based on reality, is an essential component of leadership." Advocates of enabling leadership, on the other hand, have been just as adamant. "This business is large and complex and there isn't any one of us who can have all the answers," said one executive. "I've worked hard to hire really smart people, and I listen to them."

The simple fact is that both viewpoints are valid, but neither is complete. No one can truly lead without making his or her presence felt, taking stands, setting high expectations, and making tough calls, but that leadership would be hollow and ineffective without the ability to delegate responsibility, seek others' input, show appreciation, and provide support.

Strategic and Operational Leadership

Jerry Hunt, former editor of the scientific journal *Leadership Quarterly*, has estimated that 90 percent of leadership research has been concerned with some form of the forceful/enabling dynamic. On the other hand, there has been relatively little scholarly study of the relationship between strategic leadership and operational leadership. To the extent that they have been explored, the two types are usually portrayed as completely different brands of leadership belonging to distinctly different types of leader.

One of many studies to draw this conclusion was conducted at Dow Chemical in 2003 by two Central Michigan University researchers. They compared two key roles in creating a new business—the "ideator," who comes up with the idea, and the "implementer," who makes it happen—and found that people gravitate strongly to one role or the other. Moreover, the personal profiles associated with success in each role are exact opposites. Ideators are more intellectually curious, more independent, less methodical, and less conforming. Implementers are more practical, detail-oriented, realistic, and rule-abiding.

In a recent study we conducted with Joyce Hogan, using coworker ratings on the Leadership Versatility Index and self-descriptions on the Hogan Personality Inventory, we found further evidence of the strong link between who you are and how you lead. The data revealed a strong association between strategic leadership and high scores on curiosity and open-mindedness on the one hand and low scores on a rule-abiding detail-orientation on the other. We found the opposite associations in relation to operational leadership. Forceful and enabling leadership were each related to an entirely different set of traits. Forceful leadership was associated with high scores on ambition and low scores on interpersonal sensitivity. Enabling leadership was associated with the opposite profile. Another key finding was that extreme scores on personality traits were associated with excessive use of leader behaviors— a stark reminder that those qualities that make us stand out also put us at risk.

Strategically oriented leaders are lauded for their aggressiveness and vision, but often criticized for not being sufficiently grounded in reality. Operationally oriented leaders are admired for their focus and their ability to systematically drive the organization toward its goals, but they are frequently faulted for having tunnel vision and a lack of strategic boldness. Although it may seem that that these are inherently different and mutually exclusive kinds of leaders, they are in truth prime examples of lopsided leadership. They are leaders who overuse one set of strengths at the expense of underusing others.

Once again, "strategic" and "operational" are broad categories that can be broken down into specific pairs of smaller-scope behaviors that can be virtues, or vices if overdone. Strategic leaders tend to focus on setting direction, growing or improving the organization, and driving innovation, whereas operational leaders tend to focus on execution, efficiency and capacity, and orderly process. And again, each of these leadership virtues can be turned into vices when taken to unnecessary extremes.

Consider the case of Pete Hill. As a new general manager, he had a great ability to "get under the hood" and absorb a mountain of practical knowledge. Focus, organization, and process discipline were his trademarks. He communicated his plans and

Table 2.2 Virtues and Vices of Strategic and Operational Leadership

Forceful		Enabling	
Vices	Virtues	Virtues	Vices
Head in the clouds	Direction	Execution	Tunnel vision
Eyes bigger than stomach	Growth	Efficiency	Too restrictive and cost-conscious
Fixing what isn't broken	Innovation	Order	Rigidly process-oriented

expectations in great detail and in short, punchy sentences. However, his tightly structured way of running things went hand in hand with his tendency to cut off discussion of new ideas, and his knack for focus often morphed into a failure to take a broad-enough or long-enough view. Leaders like Pete run two risks, one to their organization's ability to evolve and another to their own ability to rise above middle-management.

In contrast, there are managers, though in the minority, whose strategic proclivities are dangerously overdeveloped. Take Sam Menza, who in his mid-30s had been promoted to general manager of a big company largely on the strength of his strategic brilliance. His visionary bent impressed colleagues and clients alike, who repeatedly referred to him as a "cerebral" leader and a "fast synthesizer." Within months of his arrival, the company made a major acquisition that would never have occurred if it were not for him. However, because he had come to executive leadership so early in his career, he lacked critical experience in operations. Worse yet, he saw it as drudgery. He ignored a chorus of voices in his feedback report that begged him to pay more attention to detail, saying, "The big picture is more important and has more leverage than the day-to-day." That is a damaging posture for any leader to take. Menza was unintentionally but unmistakably telling about three-fourths of his organization that what they do doesn't really matter that much.

29

In the final analysis, a leader has to have both a long-term *and* a short-term orientation, both a broad *and* a detailed view of the organization. He or she has to track trends both outside *and* inside the organization, set direction *and* drive for results, think out of the box *and* employ tight discipline to get things done. None of these can be either/or choices. First-rate leadership, in other words, demands versatility.

The saga of Steve Jobs and John Sculley at Apple provides a classic illustration. Perhaps the most incandescent visionary of the computer age, Jobs defined Apple and its aesthetic ever since he cofounded the company in 1976. Nevertheless, when company president and cofounder Mike Markkula sought to leave his post in 1983, he believed—for good reason by all accounts—that Jobs, who was all of 28 years old, lacked the discipline and temperament not to mention the managerial experience needed to succeed him in the day-to-day running of the company. Instead, he hired Sculley, then president of PepsiCo, for the job. Though Sculley had no experience in the computer industry, Markkula and others believed that his demonstrated abilities in a more conventional consumer business would not only solidify Apple's marketing and operations, but also give the company an image of greater stability. Even Jobs himself bought into this notion and personally recruited Sculley.

For the first couple of years of his tenure, Sculley fulfilled that promise. True to his reputation as an unparalleled mass marketer, he built Apple into a household name and grew the company significantly. However, a power struggle between Jobs and Sculley soon arose, and by 1985 the board of directors lost patience and stripped Jobs of all operational responsibilities. After Jobs' bid to replace Sculley in 1986 was rejected, he left Apple to found NeXT Computer. It was then that Sculley's lack of product vision caught up with him. He championed the ill-fated Newton handheld computer and he allowed product lines to proliferate. With the resulting diffusion of focus, the engineering department degenerated into warring, paranoid fiefdoms. Despite having matured the company operationally and overseen its growth from $600 million a year to more than $8 billion, Apple's stock was still trading at about the same price. Sculley's strategic missteps ended his tenure in 1993.

When Apple purchased NeXT in 1996, Jobs returned and soon became Apple's interim CEO. But his focus was different this time. He immediately concentrated on returning Apple to profitability by terminating a number of languishing and ill-fated projects. Eventually dropping the "interim" from his title in 2000, Jobs led Apple's return to cutting-edge dominance with elegantly designed and cleverly branded home-run products such as the iPod, iPhone, and iPad.

In a recent and remarkably frank interview, Sculley offered this observation: "Looking back, it was a big mistake that I was ever hired as CEO. All the design ideas were clearly Steve's. The one who should really be given credit for all that stuff while I was there is Steve. I'm convinced that if Steve hadn't come back when he did Apple would have been history. It would have been gone, absolutely gone." Seemingly implicit in Sculley's assessment of his own tenure is the idea that he himself was too much the marketing guy, too much the business guy, and not enough of a visionary or high-tech products guy to have succeeded on his own at Apple. What he may or may not have realized, however, is that Jobs' messianic emphasis on innovation and design had been equally over-the-top and equally ill-suited to running Apple during the '80s when it desperately needed operational stability and structure to execute on the vision.

In Jobs' second tour with Apple, he was clearly no longer the one-dimensional visionary who founded the company. His experiences since then—failure at NeXt to win a market for his computer and success at Pixar by taking a higher level role made him a more versatile leader capable of blending strategic and operational imperatives. It is said that although he had lost none of his fervor for innovation and design, he came to regard delivering working products on time as equally important. This combination of visionary perspective with a drive for results is pithily captured in his oft-repeated mantra: "Real artists ship." Creativity counts only if you get the product out the door.

Versatility—The Idea and the Ideal

In the face of leadership tensions, such as those between forceful and enabling styles or strategic and operational areas of focus, many managers experience cognitive dissonance. They perceive polar opposites, not yin-and-yang complements. Rather than fall victim to a false dichotomy, however, leaders can learn to embrace both sides, even if it seems counterintuitive. They can, as Steve Jobs did, learn to overcome the paradox and become more versatile. We have worked with many executives who have done so, and it is always interesting to see their reactions when the light dawns. "You can't just be one thing," one senior manager told us. "You have to be big-picture and little-picture. You have to be a big power tool and sometimes a small screwdriver. You have to be able to zoom in and zoom out. And you can't just use one extreme quality to solve the problem."

For some, the notion of versatility conjures a vision of nondescript, homogenized leadership, always hugging the middle ground. They worry that becoming versatile will rob them of their distinctness and their edge. But such concerns are misguided. A take-charge leader needn't forfeit that capacity—only learn to use it more selectively. An empowering leader who learns to be more assertive is no less capable of empathy. All he or she gives up is *misplaced* forcefulness or *overdone* empathy. In the same vein, knowing the workings of the back office or the shop floor can only enhance one's strategic vision, and vice versa. Leaders who develop versatility don't lose their range, they enhance it.

According to the concept of yin and yang, the harmonious vibration between opposites constitutes the very stuff of existence. Versatile leadership arises from the continuous vibration between pairs of opposing impulses: to be forceful and at the same time enabling; to be visionary and at the same time to get things done. Being a versatile leader is more than having a wide repertoire of skills. It is having a wide repertoire of complementary skills that can be adapted in infinite combinations, each specific to the task at hand. The idea is to modulate or adjust your approach, including cranking up to the maximum setting if necessary. In fact, it is completely consistent with the idea of versatility to take a strength to the extreme if that's what the situation calls for, just so long as that is not your default approach to every challenge.

As a practical matter, versatility requires knowing when a certain approach is appropriate and when it is not. For instance, Steve Jobs' aggressive pursuit of excellence is legendary, and it often produced dazzling outcomes. As one story goes, just as the iPhone was about to go into production, he convened his staff and angrily pointed out scratches on the screen of a prototype. Summarily, he turned to Corning, which had a formula for glass that could not be scratched, but he was informed by CEO Wendell Weeks that because the formula had never been commercialized, it would take awhile to ramp up production. Jobs was undaunted and relentless, however, and eventually got Corning to produce the screens on his schedule.

The more versatile the leader, the more effective he or she is. We have found an exceptionally strong association between versatility scores and ratings of overall effectiveness. Versatility defined as striking a balance on both the forceful-enabling and strategic-operational dimensions accounts for about half of what separates the most effective leaders from the least effective leaders.

It is a worthwhile standard to shoot for. Even Steve Jobs, as successful as he was, seemed to realize he could have become a better leader by modulating his forcefulness and intensity. Toward the end of his life, reflecting on his infamously harsh style, he admitted, "I was hard on people sometimes, probably too hard." If he had lived longer, he might have mellowed a little without losing his edge, just as he had improved operationally. Even very successful leaders can improve by striving for versatility—maximizing the benefits of their natural strengths while containing the costs and limiting the collateral damage.

Chapter 3

Mindset

As RALPH WALDO EMERSON PUT IT, "What is life but the angle of vision? People are measured by the angle at which they look at objects." Everyone has set ways of viewing the world—themselves and their roles included. It is our worldview—our loose bundle of truths for leading and living—that drives our actions.

Imagine a leader standing alone in a room. On one wall the word "yang" is emblazoned and, on the opposite wall, "yin." The leader is facing one wall and his back is completely turned to the other. He is blind to it. For all intents and purposes, it simply does not exist for him so he makes no attempt to consider it or change his position in the room to see it. This is the very definition of "absolute lopsidedness." Now, imagine a second leader whose location in the room affords her a view of both walls. Because both are in her purview, she is inclined to consider both and, as she moves around the room, she continuously keeps both in view. This is the very definition of "versatile leadership."

Most leaders are lopsided. Early in their lives and careers, they have chosen which "wall" they will face and they are powerfully attracted to it. Lopsidedness creates a kind of elemental life force whereby everything in the leader's mindset—the mental room he occupies—is defined as either "me" or "not me." He determines what he believes to be true about leading and living and then unquestioningly clings to those "truths" under all circumstances and at all times. Those truths channel his behavior. Strong emotional forces—attractions, repulsions, ego needs—then drive behavior down those channels.

The valence of a leader's world view can be so strong that he is actually repulsed by the opposite (if it ever comes to his attention). The settings on his dials are so far off that he becomes a liability even to himself. His value and accomplishments are completely overshadowed and undermined by the toll he takes on his organization and his family's and his own well-being. This kind of leader is often infamous within his organization—a legend in his own time for all the wrong reasons.

Even highly effective leaders are governed by set ways of viewing themselves and the world that do not serve them well. Even the most clearheaded, rational managers have off in the corner of their minds little puddles of muddy thinking. One high-potential manager, for example, came out with this statement in his feedback session, "I've always believed that being effective means knowing things and getting things done." What was missing from that formulation is any notion that leadership requires working with others. Predictably, his feedback said he was not good at relationships—though very good technically and very goal-oriented. No wonder he stressed getting results above all else, to the point that he had blinders on.

Distorted beliefs are tinged, if not saturated, with anxiety. A leader's mindset throbs with desire to succeed and with fear of failure, with yearning to be "good" and horror of being "bad." A brief example: a senior manager revealed in a feedback session that he operated on the assumption that "I should know everything all the time." The word "should" hinted at the pressure this person constantly put on himself. Leaders who fall prey to this kind of emotion-laden erroneous logic are compromised in their ability to function. It throws off their form.

A leader's mindset will throw off his form just as an athlete's does. At the highest levels of sport, everyone has exceptional physical ability, but it's the inner game that makes the difference. It's the ability to be intense but not tense at the plate and in the field, the ability to put a bad play immediately out of one's mind and recover for the next play. When an athlete in his prime is off form—when the ace pitcher has control problems, the all-star shortstop mysteriously can't throw the ball to first base, or someone like Tiger Woods suddenly can't find the fairway—it is usually not because his skills have suddenly eroded. More likely, something in his psyche is impeding his ability to orchestrate those skills to their fullest expression. Among professional athletes, it is well established that a player's psychology matters.

Most leaders have no trouble seeing how the mental game makes a difference in sports. Yet somehow fewer are able to see the role and relevance of mindset in their own line of work and, in particular, in their own case. Nevertheless it is a simple, incontrovertible truth: who you are is how you lead.

What's behind Overuse?

In our experience, there are some common mindset traps.

A More-Is-Better Mentality

It never ceases to amaze us how easily leaders slip into a more-is-better mentality. A closet pride may be at work: I'm the first one to arrive in the morning and the last to leave in the evening (never mind that I'm burned out). I'm more data-oriented and analytical (never mind the analysis paralysis). I'm more candid than the rest (in reality, needlessly confrontational). I'm more principled (even though everyone else is fed up with the moralizing). I do a better job of coaching (even though ignorant of when being helpful isn't helpful).

"What do you mean?" was the retort we got when we told a manager that his coworkers' rating of him, a 5, the highest possible score, on "Drive for results," could mean he was taking it too far. He and many others consider more of a prized attribute to always be better. For them, the maximum is the optimum. No surprise, we suppose, in a land of super-sized meals and oversized vehicles. But, as Bob Kaplan's grandmother used to say, "Too much is plenty."

The human tendency to maximize is phenomenal. An executive who discovered running in her 40s made a point of logging five miles a day, no matter the weather or where she was. Eventually, it caught up with her—knee problems, then ankle tendonitis, then bursitis in her hip.

Another executive, Billy Pace, decided to teach himself how to play the piano. After a year of practicing regularly he asked his pianist friend to listen to his playing. "Great," his friend said, "but you're playing three times too fast." Billy told us, "I was looking for an affirmation that fast was good, and it wasn't."

Billy Pace valued speed at work too—absorbed input quickly, made decisions quickly, acted quickly. "Quick" could be his middle name. The problem was that he rushed decisions. Either he did not get all the input he needed and therefore sometimes made poor calls, or he didn't touch base with all the key parties and therefore ran into resistance when he tried to implement the decision. Why the rush, we asked? "Inaction is bad." In response to this curiously flat statement, we asked, "How so?" With unexpected force he exclaimed, "I need to earn this job every single day, even if it's Saturday or Sunday. I feel this need, whatever I earned yesterday I have to earn again today." Or else? "I'd stop being the provider." Then what? "The sky falls. Nuclear winter." A near violent emotional wind howls in his head and rushes his actions. His family lost everything when he was growing up. His father, the sole breadwinner, lost his job and was out of work for a long period. Now a father himself, being a good provider was freighted with significance.

A Skewed Mental Model

Imagine each person's model of leadership as a box containing circles that represent the leader's areas of responsibility. The size of each circle indicates the importance the leader places on each responsibility. Inevitably, when the leader overplays a strength, the circle corresponding to that element of leadership is grossly oversized.

In some people, the circle representing "prepare" is disproportionately large. A newly appointed head of investor relations (IR) vastly overprepared for board meetings and presentations to analysts. Before presentations he was so nervous he threw up. A colleague commented, "He feels like he has to answer every question, think of every angle, and he doesn't." Easy for an onlooker to be objective. The IR head was driven by a subjective reality—an assumption laced with fear—over which, in his first couple of years in the job, he had little control.

A grossly exaggerated sense of responsibility is another case of an oversized mindset element. Leaders with this characteristic seem to imagine themselves the mythical Atlas bearing the weight of the planet on their shoulders. Their sense of ownership greatly exceeds what is expected of them. In our experience their backgrounds all have something in common. At a young age they all lost their father—to divorce, desertion, a terminal disease, a fatal car accident. Abruptly, they were pressed into service. Even if they were under age, they got jobs to help support the family. They had household chores thrust upon them. With responsibility thrust upon them prematurely, they overlearned the lesson. "I grew up fast," they say. "Mature beyond their years," others said.

Some mothers stepped up—went to work, held the family together. Their inspiring example further reinforced the leader's sense of responsibility. Some mothers fell apart—became alcoholics, fell into depression—and the first-born had to take responsibility for his or her mother too, adding to the load and burning a still greater sense of responsibility into their brains.

A Faulty Gauge

One senior manager we worked with couldn't figure out why his staff was slow to meet his requests. We tried some role playing with him where we were cast as his direct reports. When he told us what he wanted done, he not only didn't specify a deadline, but he also spoke extremely softly. When we told him this, he specified a deadline, but only managed to raise his voice slightly. Trying a third time, he finally did speak louder and with authority. When we asked him to grade the intensity of the attempts on a scale of ten, he offered three, five, and eight. "My reading," one of us said, "was two, three, and five." He was an executive who worked hard to keep his ego in check—too hard as it turned out. He was too good at self-restraint. The calibration on his forcefulness dial was way off.

Behind his overdone self-restraint was a fear of self-promotion. He told us he found it "distasteful when people put themselves forward." A voice in his head yelled at him, "Don't talk about yourself all the time. Don't think that what's good for you is right for everybody. Don't make other people feel small by making yourself big." His intense aversion to anything vaguely resembling egotism blurred his reading of the line separating healthy self-assertion and boastfulness. To make sure he didn't cross the line, he stood much farther away from it than necessary. His lack of vocal power was accompanied by a lack of communicative power. He failed to keep top management fully informed about his activities and accomplishments, and thereby undermined his credibility.

For that manager and many others like him, overdoing or underdoing are not simply the result of a cognitive inability to read one's behavioral "dial." The poor calibration comes from distorted notions and uncontrolled emotion that cause them to wildly overcompensate.

What's behind Lopsidedness?

Lopsided leadership in all its forms stems from a bias toward one side of leadership and a prejudice against the other side. The leader identifies strongly with one worldview while at the same time thinking the less of the opposite.

The prejudice against one side is not usually overt, but it is very clear in subtext. One senior leader who overweighted driving for results and underweighted personal connection referred to relationship-building as "schmoozing." A dead give-away. Another executive who had a gift for visionary leadership but no taste for operational responsibility tipped his hand with the phrase "operational gruel." In cases like these, leaders genuinely believe their view is a perfectly good rationale when in fact it is pure rationalization. A blind spot.

Lopsided leaders can identify with a side of leadership to the point where they don't know there is an opposite side. Their view of that aspect of leadership is one-sided. They don't think of it as part of a duality. When asked point-blank to identify it, they are at a loss. An upper-level manager who believed strongly in communicating openly with his team sometimes passed on sensitive information intended for his eyes or ears only, to the dismay of senior management. When we asked him to identify a strength that is the opposite of openness, he couldn't come up with it. "Discretion," we said. Genuinely surprised he said, "Oh, I hadn't thought of that."

A highly principled manager, active in his church, practiced service-oriented leadership with a missionary zeal that left him exhausted, overweight, out of shape, and, if he were honest with himself, resentful. Yet there was no place in his mind for what might be the useful opposite of being service-oriented. He bridled when we suggested "serving yourself" and told us that "selfishness is unacceptable." He could not see that there is a big difference between taking care of oneself and being selfish, and it took some time for him to accept that serving oneself is a means to serving others. Cherishing one truth can blind the leader to the opposing truth.

In bending over backward to avoid one thing, the leader can inadvertently overdo something else. We see this syndrome in overly zealous high achievers who skimp on the social side of their job. In the typical profile, they excelled as students and got richly reinforced for that. For one reason or another they were less successful with friends and suffered over that. In one scenario, circumstances put them on the margin and contributed to their lack of social success. They came from a family whose race or religion or country of origin made them a minority and put them at a disadvantage. Or they came from a poor family and had to work full-time to help make ends meet. That left them with little time to socialize with their peers. The pattern set in childhood persisted once they became managers. They gravitated to what they did well and gravitated away from what they didn't think they were good at it.

One executive very strongly identified with being a general manager and just as clearly distanced himself from the technical functions and technical staff. This was puzzling because he had an undergraduate degree in engineering and a graduate degree in computer science and had begun his career in a technical function. Once, in a reflective mood, he admitted to us that he polarized technological depth and management breadth. "It's true," he said, "my most tense relationships are with the technical people. Clearly, I have distaste for the techno-nerd."

A glimpse into his background told the story. His negative associations went all the way back to childhood. "I was an ungainly kid, on the dorky side, always a little overweight, not good at sports, and I was teased a lot." He adapted by becoming "an academic kid." That brought him success but also fed into his sense of himself as marginal. He came to equate depth of knowledge with narrowness, which he associated with somehow being less valuable. "At some level I still think of myself that way," he said. In an attempt to redefine himself, he passed up a chance to go to MIT and instead went to a highly selective liberal arts college where he was exposed to a wide range of talented peers. "I think it triggered a desire in me to be broader," he acknowledged. "A lot of the things I've done in my career have been an attempt to be broad. That's why I prefer general management to technology. It's more worldly."

The source of lopsidedness may run deep. William Lessor had what seemed to his team an insatiable and unaccountable appetite for up-to-the-minute knowledge of the business. Behind his appetite for information and detail was a shadowy truth: he didn't think he was smart. He told us, "I'm afraid that if I'm meeting with my team or even people lower in the organization and something comes up that I'm not aware of, they'll think I'm stupid." Fear of inadequacy was the culprit. Arming himself to the teeth with detail was a way of protecting himself.

The same fear of inadequacy threw off his leadership in another way. It caused him to shrink from the strategic part of his job. Thus this fear flung him in two opposing directions—avoidance of strategic work and ardor for detail.

The idea that he was not smart had been imprinted on him early. He was third-born in his family and, when he was young, his two older siblings always got straight A's. They went to prestigious colleges. They were "the smart ones." Unlike his brothers he didn't apply himself in school and naturally his grades suffered. In his child's mind his grades indicated lack of ability when in fact they reflected lack of effort. A teacher's gratuitous comment cemented his inferiority complex: "I had a teacher in third grade who told me I'd never amount to anything. Yes, that hurt, absolutely. And it still has a strong influence." The little-known college he went to stood as further evidence to him that he had a second-rate mind. What's striking is that his faulty reasoning remained intact like a fossilized insect far into adulthood. All these years, he had kept his sense of inadequacy a deep, dark secret—a secret even to himself. It was only when we questioned his reasoning that he saw how he had confused lack of effort with lack of ability. His confusion on this critical feature of his self-view is a good example of how a painful, anachronistic idea of oneself can live on for decades.

Lopsided leaders waste inordinate amounts of energy on self-concern. Energy that would be better spent on productive activity is sadly diverted into ego protection. We've seen how far out of his way William Lessor went to protect his ego. Lopsided leaders are overanxious not to feel small, inadequate, helpless, or worthless. They do everything in their power to avoid or shut down situations that pose that threat. If they doubt themselves socially, they avoid informal conversation. If they doubt themselves intellectually, they avoid conceptual work. If they fear conflict, they shut down debate. They are acutely sensitive to their psychological safety.

Inordinate energy is also channeled into ego gratification. It's the boundless appetite to make a splash, stand out in a crowd, be admired. It can lead individuals to inflate their own importance, steal the limelight, take credit due others. It was said about a leader, "He spends too much time managing perceptions. It ought to be 5 percent and I think it's more like 20 percent."

The Hero Syndrome

Although the one-dimensional, over-the-top intensity of lopsidedness is the result of a flawed mindset and overcompensating behavior, it is often seen by others as heroic leadership. Whatever these leaders think of themselves, others invest them with nearly superhuman qualities. Indeed, people such as Rick Spire, Carla Middleton, Steve Jobs, and Jeff Skilling are often blessed with heroic qualities—raw talent, vast energy, and burning ambition—but it is a mixed blessing. Their risk/reward ratio is dangerously high. They overleverage themselves: everything revolves around them and all roads lead to them. Up to a point, that works because they bring so much to the table. Beyond that point, however, they become like Icarus, whose wings melted when he flew too close to the sun. The risks they run, both to their organization and to themselves, become intolerable and destructive. A certain number of them become the Jeffrey Skillings of the world, more a curse than a blessing, more cursed than blessed.

Ironically, the more capable and heroic the leader, the more lopsidedness presents a serious downside risk. To visualize what we mean, take a look at one leader's "versatility wheel," a graphic representation we use to show a leader's tendency to do too much or too little with regard to each of the two major leadership dualities. A case in point: Janice Herald, the CEO of a company owned by a private equity firm.

Janice's wheel shows how her coworkers rate her on each of the 12 characteristics or behaviors that constitute the six main sub-dualities—listens/declares, pushes/supports, and so on. The ratings are compiled

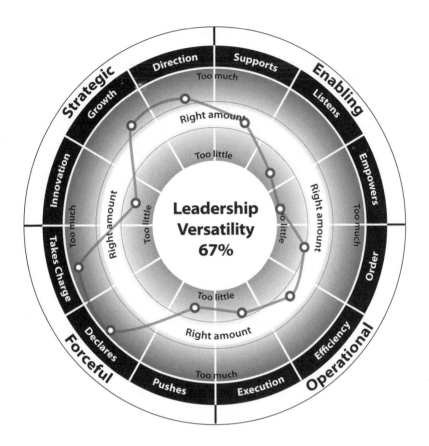

using the Leadership Versatility Index; the small circles in each "slice of the pie" represent her average ratings in that category. The percentage in the center is an index of how many times she was rated to have the "right amount" of any of the 12 characteristics. (A percentage in the 60s is the equivalent of a grade of D.) With the dots of her ratings connected, you can see the bulges. This is extreme lopsidedness.

Like other heroic types, Janice Herald was dealt a strong hand. The problem was that she overplayed it. That strong tendency is reflected in her extreme too-much scores on "takes charge" and "declares." A gifted talker with a razor-sharp mind, she could dazzle everyone in meetings. But she took more than her share of air time, even in informal conversations, and sucked the oxygen out of the tent. She was clear and decisive and made up her mind easily, but she made too many decisions unilaterally. "Too much Janice" is how her staff and her peers described it.

On the other hand there were corresponding areas where there was "too little Janice." Although she demanded the world of herself, she often failed to demand the best of others (see her too-little score on "pushes"). Because of her dominating personality she didn't empower or listen enough.

Janice's extreme lopsided behavior could be traced to her skewed and rigid mindset. In short, she saw the world in heroic and unyielding terms. "I believe there are real leaders and there are posers," she related. She viewed performance, hers and everyone else's, as either awesome or awful, black or white. "I have a bit of hero worship," she told us. She had more than a bit. She put her high-achieving, socially prominent parents on a pedestal. She revered certain of her highly placed mentors. Further reflecting her hero mentality, she consumed a steady diet of books, films, and sporting events that featured conquering heroes. Her mentality was also on display in her own recreational heroics: she was a dedicated and successful triathlete.

Her lopsidedness also had its roots in the forces that drove her. Her immense need for control was not an end in itself, but rather a visceral desire for a sense of worth on a grand scale—a glorious career, a crowning point that would preclude all debate. As Napoleon summed it up, "A great reputation is a great noise. The more that is made, the farther it is heard." Janice came to recognize her irresistible urge to garner credit and the fall-out from that urge: "I'm too concerned about my need to achieve to be able to share with others."

Janice Herald's dread of failure added fuel to the fire of her ambition. Fear of never amounting to anything preyed on her mind. "I can't even watch movies about losers," she said. But it went deeper than that. Her plight was existential angst, existential anguish. Her own mortality was never far from her mind. She could not abide being limited, being finite, in any way. It's no wonder she did a poor job keeping herself in bounds.

Janice's frenzied egocentrism made her a deeply flawed leader who was in danger of self-destruction. When her 360 feedback reflected that fact, she understandably took it hard. "It sucks to be sitting here with this much career success and get this kind of feedback." She came around when she realized that to preserve her heroic identity she had to stop blindly defending it. She had to become more versatile. "I do want to improve," she said. "I want to be a better person, leader, and mother."

Recently, she took up Tai Chi and her instructor immediately picked up on how tightly wound she was. As her neck jutted forward, straining and incompatible with the seamless flowing movement that is the essence of Tai Chi, he told her, "You are so intent on doing this well that your body is stiff. It lacks flexibility. There is so much tension you can't possibly flow." There could have been no better metaphor for her limitations as a leader and the challenges of her road ahead.

For better and for worse, who you are is how you lead.

Chapter 4

Dialing Back

LEFT TO THEIR OWN DEVICES, most leaders won't work on their mindset. They are more conditioned to work on their behavior itself—their form—than on the psychology behind it. They are used to getting feedback on their behavior, coming up with a plan to change it, and trying to behave in the prescribed new way. But they leave mindset leverage on the table. It only makes sense, however, that you address what is inside your head that threw off your form in the first place, the warped views and emotional forces that result in overdoing it and lopsidedness. As Einstein put it, "We can't solve problems using the same kind of thinking we used when we created them."

Mindset change is not just an enabler of behavior change. Mindset change and behavior change have equal standing. They are parallel tracks toward improvement and need to be given equal standing in any action plan. Your best chance of making change stick is to do both the outer work and the inner work of improving. The complementary efforts can be summarized in a simple one-by-two matrix. For instance, the hyperintense, fastball-throwing leader mentioned in this book's introduction framed his improvement plan this way:

Behavior Change	Mindset Change
Stop overwhelming people.	I don't have to give up my fast-ball. I just don't need to throw it all the time.

Mindset change is difficult for most leaders because it requires them to uncover the subconscious defense mechanisms that underpin their overcompensating behaviors. They then have to rectify their thinking and dial back those behaviors. In the go-all-out world that most leaders inhabit, they are far more comfortable with behavioral change that requires them to do more of something, not less. Their default mindset is to strive, work hard, meet the challenge, and exceed expectations. To them, "dialing up" feels right. Although dialing up is part of overcoming lopsidedness and is discussed in the next chapter, it is not the focus of this book; there are lots of books that tell you how to overcome your weaknesses. Our primary concern is with the more nuanced, less acknowledged, and in some ways more difficult task of dialing back your strengths.

The notion that one can try *too* hard is counterintuitive for many leaders. It's not easy for them to get used to the idea that they can be too invested, too attached, or too intense—that beyond a certain point more is not better, it's actually worse. The thought of backing off is heresy for most, but that is exactly what they need to do to improve their performance. "It came as a surprise to me that something you pride yourself in, something you do well, can turn into a weakness," one executive told us. "At first I wanted to discount the feedback, but then I started to wonder, how could I bring that back to the center without losing the strength? How could I adjust?"

Despite what you may think, you can learn to dial back your strengths, even those that you have come to rely heavily upon and may regard as the keys to your success thus far. The good news is that excess is a cloud with a silver lining. Within your excesses lie all the ability you will ever need. All you have to do is learn to regulate them better. In this chapter, we lay out an approach for doing so. It requires that you get comfortable with working on yourself, from the outside in and from the inside out. It is tough work, but it is effective. The only question you need to answer is, how committed are you to success?

The Outer Game: Working on Your Behavior

The behavioral approach is a very effective and direct way for leaders to improve, and there are a number of useful techniques for doing so.

First of all, you can't very well dial back if you don't know what you overdo. There is only one way to find out and that is to ask, in conversation or in a formal evaluation: do I take any of my strengths too far? Because people are used to thinking in terms of shortcomings, you may find that your question puts them at a loss. So explain: "You know, too much of a good thing." You can also use a feedback survey to learn about what you overdo, but because the typical survey relies on a five-point scale that assumes more is better, you will have to make sure you include a way for coworkers to indicate where you overdo it. Our 360 survey, the Leadership Versatility Index, has coworkers indicate whether you do too much, the right amount, or too little of a given behavior—relative to your job and your organization.

Once managers are made aware of what they overdo, those who succeed at dialing back often use the phrase, "I caught myself." Catching yourself is essentially an act of awareness coupled with willpower. You can become attuned to the signs that you are about to go too far and rein yourself in before it happens. For example, someone who has been made aware that his penchant for directness can cross the line into offensiveness can learn to be alert to the stimulus that triggers that response. Often the signs are physical. One manager discovered that his left leg would begin to bounce moments before he made a too-pointed comment in a meeting. Another could feel his face flush moments before he was about to let a subordinate have it for letting him down. Another, who was told that his customary exuberance could be overwhelming, realized that in such moments he often felt like "a spring wound too tight."

Those signals, physical and emotional, are useless if you don't tune into them. Many leaders do not. As our colleague Lawrence Stibbards says, "We live in our heads." So in striving to restrain yourself, it helps to get better acquainted with your moment-to-moment emotional life and more conversant in the language of your body.

If you learn to recognize the signs, you can press the pause button to give yourself a moment to choose an alternative to your customary knee-jerk reaction. The idea is to interrupt the reflex. You can dissipate the urge to blurt something out by writing down what you were about to say. If you find yourself wound too tight at the start of a meeting, you can make a practice of taking deep breaths to calm down. It is learning to do what great performers in any line of work do: slow down the action so that you can, in a

Malcolm Gladwell "blink," modulate your natural reflex reactions.

Another aid to dialing back is to choose a brief directive, simply worded, to carry around in your head. A "swing thought" is a golfer's term for a single correction to your form that you keep in mind as you stand over the ball. The idea is that to try to make several adjustments at once is a setup for failure. A swing thought keys on a very specific single behavior that stands for the overall shift you are seeking to make. Carla Middleton, you will recall, was all too ready to take center stage, but learned that she inadvertently cut people off mid-sentence when she thought she knew what they were getting at. Her swing thought became simply, "Let the other person finish." Although there was a lot more to temper in her overbearing nature, letting people complete their thoughts was a good start and a good reminder of her larger goal.

A swing thought has to be more than a technical pointer or a bloodless technique. It must be grounded in a true feeling and realization. One manager had just such a startling realization when we engaged him in some role playing. Although there is a time and a place to defer to your superiors, he was just too good at it, to the point of subservience. When we asked him to act out with us how he might make a proposal to the top team, he actually genuflected. The realization of his obsequiousness repulsed him. The swing thought he chose: "Not on bended knee!"

A middle manager, who regularly worked on his form both as a leader and as a golfer, concluded: "Positive swing thoughts are much better than negative ones. A negative swing thought such as 'Don't try to crush the ball' or 'Don't move your head' tells you what not to do and focuses your attention on not messing up. A positive swing thought focuses you on doing the right thing to improve your game."

Adopting a regimen is another highly effective way to dial back a strength. Even a sincere ambition to improve will fall apart if it is not buttressed by discipline, and routine and a regimen provides both. Just as we were told as children, just as we tell our own children, practice makes perfect. To rein in a tendency to give her staff too much autonomy, one manager set aside "office hours"—thirty minutes for each direct report—every Tuesday afternoon. She had imposed a structure that initially took her out of her comfort zone, but eventually expanded that comfort zone. Using this simple regimen, she got in the habit of giving her people better direction.

Managers driven to work endless hours can also benefit from imposing formal restraints on themselves. One individual made a commitment to leave the office at 5:30 P.M. twice a week when he wasn't traveling so that he could have dinner with his wife and two young daughters. He told his assistant, so she could shoo him out of the office at 5:15. He told his wife in advance, so she wouldn't fall off her chair when he walked in the door. How did he do? He couldn't sustain the twice-a-week regimen, but he did institutionalize a weekly practice. It may not seem like much, but it was a vast improvement over never getting home for dinner at all.

Another manager had always believed that his nervous energy and near-frantic way of going about his job were the keys to his success. The last thing he wanted to do was tamper with a winning formula, but his overintensity was beginning to take a toll. In an effort to be less tense, less agitated, he decided to learn to meditate. He played a compact disc that walked him through a step-by-step 20-minute program. For the first time, he began to experience what it felt like to be relaxed. The regimen worked. He bought an audio version of Dale Carnegie's *How to Stop Worrying and Start Living*, replete with instructive stories of people facing serious problems who nevertheless learned to relax. Over and over on his drive back and forth to work, for months on end, he listened to the book. "When I get to the end of the book, I start over," he said. How is that for intense?! But it helped. He was better able to put in perspective situations that would have gotten to him in the past.

A formal relaxation technique belongs in the toolkit of every leader. In their *Harvard Business Review* article, "The Making of a Corporate Athlete," Jim Loehr and Tony Schwartz contend that the regular practice of meditation quiets the mind and creates mental space for ideas to simply come to you. No fancy technique is necessary. You can pick it up by reading an article or listening to an audio recording. Once it's in your repertoire, you can pull it out any time you are getting carried away, at work or at home. Even five minutes can calm you down.

The key to successful behavior change through any kind of "outer work" is consistency. Through repetition you recondition yourself.

The Inner Game: Working on Your Mindset

As important as the "outer work" is, however, it is not enough. Though many subscribe to the adage that says it is "better to act your way into a new way of thinking than think your way into a new way of acting," that is patently one-sided and simply untrue. It is better to do both. Your best chance of actually making an improvement is to come at it simultaneously from the outside in and from the inside out.

Despite what you may think, your mental tendencies *can* be reformed, or at least managed better, to reinforce your actions. The brain's plasticity makes that possible. It is "a structure weak enough to yield to an influence but strong enough not to yield all at once," wrote William James, who in 1890 authored of one of the first comprehensive books on psychology.

Many habits of mind are tacit. You half-know them yet have never quite articulated them to yourself or out loud. However, with a little help, most leaders are quite capable of having epiphanies, little bursts of awareness that make it more likely they will be able to catch themselves. Sometimes a nudge is all it takes.

It took only a few-minute exchange for one manager to uncover the mental driver just beneath the surface of an undesirable habit: "Come to think of it," she said, "I spend too much time on emails because I want them to be perfect. No need to do that."

With a little prodding, another executive discovered an underlying ego need: "If one of my people asks a question, I'll immediately give him the answer, rather than turn the question back to him to get him to think about it. I see now that when I answer the question, it's selfish. I'm meeting my need to be productive and to show him that I'm smart."

And another quickly put his finger on a deep driver of his high-revving leadership style: "I don't trust myself, so I'm constantly having to prove my worth. Internally, I'm constantly churning, telling myself I've got to turn the intensity up."

For other individuals, it's a struggle to get past a blind spot. Recall Sam Menza, who focused much harder on strategy than on the operational part of his job because he felt "the bigger picture was more important." Even when we showed him the consensus feedback from his direct reports saying that he needed to be more detail-oriented and more engaged operationally, he wasn't influenced. He equated attention to detail with being bogged down in it and wanted no part of that. In some cases, the roots of overuse are shallow and easily pulled up. But in cases like Sam's, the root mass of distorted thinking has wrapped itself around the individual's core sense of self and is not easily removed.

The reality is that the halls of every organization are littered with stories of nagging performance problems that have persisted over the years despite everyone's best efforts. Think how many times you yourself have made a genuine commitment to improve only to come away disappointed. The research tells us that an iterative cycle of reflection and action is required to achieve lasting change: insight begets action begets insight begets action. The inner work and the outer work must be done together and continuously to overcome the embedded effects of overdone strengths and lopsidedness.

Fixing Overuse

You will remember that William Lessor had long suffered from an inferiority complex about his intellect that mired him in tactical detail. Fear drove his hyperattention to detail: "I'm afraid that if I'm meeting with my team or even people lower in the organization and something comes up that I'm not aware of, they'll think I'm stupid." He was afraid of being stupid even though he was widely viewed as plenty smart. When we first asked him to make a list of his strengths, he did not include any version of the word "smart." During the feedback session, we called his attention to the omission and suggested he add "smart" to his list, but he could not do it, even after he had received formal feedback from coworkers that included appreciation of his intellect. When he became aware of this blind spot, he formulated an action plan for change, a simple two-pronged assault:

Behavior Change	Mindset Change
Dial back on tactical detail.	I may not be the smartest person in the room, but I'm smart enough to do my job.

Two years later, he had made progress that was clearly reflected in the high praise that his team and the board heaped on him in the follow-up report. In a kind of graduation ceremony he took out his original list and hand-entered "smart." Although his sense of self-worth remained a work in progress, thereafter, when he tackled strategic issues and began to doubt his ability to handle them, he was able to catch himself, banish the thought, and get down to work.

Leaders often have trouble backing off an over-used behavior because they see it as an all-or-nothing choice. "If I stop being so forceful, will I lose my edge?" "If I stop being so nice to people, will I turn into an SOB?" Faced with feedback that indicated she needed to dial back her tendency to dominate people and situations, Carla Middleton reacted this way: "When I first got the feedback, I took it to mean that I needed to throw an on-off switch. But now I see there are more than two levels. It's more like a volume control. It's continuous." The idea of a dial frees you to fine-tune your strength without any danger of losing it completely. One leader captured the dynamic well: "At the start of the process I worried that the good part would weaken. But no, only the bad part weakens and the good part strengthens." Truth is, most people could not lose the positive aspects of their strength even if they tried to.

Reining in an excessively used strength doesn't mean you forsake it. You just learn to be selective with it. The "fastball-throwing" leader, a baseball fan, told us the story of Sandy Koufax, the brilliant Los Angeles Dodgers pitcher who didn't become great until he stopped throwing his fastball so hard and so often. Koufax came into his own when he took his catcher's advice to "stop trying to blow the ball by the hitters," to "try more curves and change-ups." The Dodgers' manager, Walter Alston, said that Koufax was less effective when he pitched with "all muscle and no finesse, trying to use 100 percent of his strength." Once Koufax learned to govern his power, using "90 percent of it in a steady, rhythmical pattern," and throwing the right pitch in the right situation, he was able to pitch no-hitters in four consecutive seasons culminating with a perfect game in 1965.

Another of the main driving forces behind overuse is perfectionism, a common affliction of leaders. The best becomes the enemy of the good. Psychoanalytic thinker Karen Horney spoke of this as the "tyranny of the shoulds." Rigidly high expectations and fear of falling short can bully a person into a lack of modulation, which ultimately can be self-defeating.

Andre Agassi, the eight-time Grand Slam tennis champion, revealed in his recent autobiography that he had always hated tennis during his career because of the constant pressure it exerted on him. His friend and later coach, Brad Gilbert, told him: "You don't have to be the best in the world every time you go out there. Right now, by trying for the perfect shot with every ball, you're stacking the odds against yourself. When you chase perfection, you're chasing something that doesn't exist. You're making everyone around you miserable. You're making yourself miserable." Agassi later said: "I find peace in his claim that perfectionism is voluntary. I always assumed perfectionism was an inborn part of me." Once he internalized Gilbert's guidance, Agassi adjusted his mental and physical game and went on to win six of his eight Grand Slams.

The first step toward lessening the tyranny of the shoulds is to, as Agassi did, stand outside of your tightly wrapped system of thought. To help Carla Middleton take that step, we guided her through a process devised by developmental psychologist Robert Kegan at Harvard. The foundation of Kegan's process is making specific commitments to change. Carla's commitment was to give other people a chance to express their views. The process soon revealed, however, that Carla had a competing subconscious commitment, a deep and longstanding need to "not be unsure, to not be lost or out of control." It emerged that when she feels out of control the whole foundation of her efficacy crumbles: "I don't achieve results. I'm not successful. It's a disaster." Subconscious, self-protective, competing commitments account for why so many well-intended efforts to change don't pan out. They constitute the resistance to change that, unless dealt with directly, will defeat your attempt to improve.

An invaluable tool for modulating an overplayed strength is positive feedback, plenty of it. For years we have deliberately used it as leverage for development, to correct a deeply held misperception or allay fears of inadequacy, and we have repeatedly seen it work. It's not true what managers everywhere think, that it's negative feedback that is useful, that it is the criticism they can do something about.

Billy Peoples, widely admired as cooperative, decent, and honorable, nevertheless worried that he wasn't enough of those things. Hearing this, a peer pointed out to him: "You carry around a bucket of 'good-guy capital' that is so full it spills out. And your 'bad-guy capital' bucket is empty." In other words, Billy had plenty of leeway to take the unpopular stands that he had habitually shied away from. Hearing a peer dispel one of his embedded fears helped free Peoples from its grip.

Positive feedback has the power to hit home in ways that negative feedback does not. One senior manager had a bad habit of being rough on people who didn't "get it right away." He received sharply negative, though anonymous, feedback from his staff—many said he "berated" them—which certainly got his attention but, strangely, didn't change his behavior. However, a very different kind of feedback that struck *beneath* the surface of his behavior did get through: his staff rated him as "off-the-charts" smart. After he read that section of the report, he just sat there, saying nothing. This was completely out of character for this animated person who was never at a loss for words. Finally, we asked for his reaction. "Sobered," he replied, an answer we were completely unprepared for. He realized that his superior intelligence was what made him impatient with people who weren't quite as quick on their feet. Immediately after the session, his offensive behavior essentially stopped. It was as if that way of relating to people dropped out of his behavioral vocabulary.

You can clamp down on bad behavior but that's merely treating the symptom. Better to go after the root cause, which often turns out to be a failure to recognize the extent of an asset. As Peter Drucker said, "Most American managers don't know what their strengths are. When you ask them, they look at you with a blank stare." However, when their strengths are reflected back to them in stark feedback, it makes a strong impression. They are made to regard the impact of those strengths for both good and ill.

To underestimate yourself is to risk needlessly overcompensating and perverting your capabilities by taking them too far. When you recognize the full extent of your ability and stop worrying that you are not good enough, you will be less likely to take that strength to a counterproductive extreme. By stripping away the excess surrounding a strength, you are left with the effective core.

Fixing Lopsidedness

As the novelist F. Scott Fitzgerald put it, "The test of a first-rate intelligence is the ability to hold two opposed ideas in mind at the same time and still retain the ability to function." That bit of wisdom captures what it takes to escape lopsidedness in both thought and action.

Given that lopsidedness is defined by overemphasizing one leadership approach and underemphasizing its complement, the remedy, from a strictly behavioral standpoint, is a single two-fisted action: place one hand on each dial and simultaneously turn one down and the other up. At the same time, from the mindset perspective, the challenge is to uncover the root of the polarization and reconcile it. You must cease to define one approach as your truth, your thesis, and the other as your antithesis. Your perception then changes from this versus that to this *with* that—giving you two valid, mutually reinforcing ways of operating.

Take the example of Sally Lowe, a functional manager who was highly regarded for her level of skill and for holding herself to a high standard. However, her performance suffered from not holding her people to the same standard of excellence. If direct reports missed a deadline or submitted subpar work, she let them off the hook. Each time it happened, she had a bad taste in her mouth but swallowed it. Her organization's performance suffered and so did the morale of the team's high performers.

In her own defense, Sally would extol the virtues of being nice to people, what she strongly believed was the socially desirable way to be. Instead of realizing that one could strive to treat people well and at the same time hold them accountable, she polarized the behaviors into good and bad. When we asked her to define the opposite of being nice, she replied "being a jerk." We asked, "Is the opposite of nice alien to you?" "Yes, it's alien," she said.

In later discussion, she was able to put her finger on the reason for this: "The need to be liked has too big a place for me," she admitted, making a downward motion with her arm, indicating that it needed to be reduced. She said that if she were to tell someone she was dissatisfied with his or her performance "I'm afraid I wouldn't be liked. It's tangled." Like so many of us, Sally's subconscious need dictated her counterproductive behavior, which she then rationalized by deeming it "right" and the alternative "wrong." As a wise writer said, "Fear robs people of the ability to deal with contradiction, and reduces them to black-and-white thinking."

Sally Lowe's aversion to being "pushy" started in childhood. She had a dominating older brother who was forever having run-ins with their father and at times bullied her. Instinctively, she gravitated away from her brother's example. It was safer to keep down, to "lie low." Her inhibition accompanied her into adulthood: "Twenty years ago, just asserting myself in a store was intimidating," she said. Making the connection to her childhood helped her to see that a pattern that had been shaped by circumstances could conceivably now be reshaped.

First, she made a dual commitment to dial up her tough side and to dial down her supportive side by simply behaving differently—acting her way into a new way of thinking. At the same time, she resolved that she needed to change her mindset: "I see that this shift has to do with reconciling being demanding with being nice. Right now those two things don't join."

Behavior Change	Mindset Change
Be good to people and also hold them to the same high standard you hold yourself to.	Holding people accountable is not incompatible with treating them well.

Part of Sally's mindset change entailed readjusting her sense of her professional self. "I don't treat myself as a big shot," she said. "I will generally scale down." To assert herself more with staff, however, meant she needed to assume a bigger presence, in effect filling out her managerial role or, as her husband told her, "taking advantage of what you're entitled to."

When attempting to improve managerially, it always helps to make a parallel change outside of work. As a long-time and still devoted tennis player, Sally knew she overrelied on a finesse game, specializing in a backhand shot with lots of spin on the ball. She never went for the jugular. She decided to work on her forehand put-away shot, saying, "I'd like to hit harder. I'd like to have more impact. I've been overcompensating with my backhand." Attempting to make that shift on the court reinforced her effort to make the same shift in the office.

Using Counterweights

Changing yourself is an admirable exercise in self-control. But it is wise to also employ counterweights—processes or people—to aid your efforts. As one senior manager with a strong personality learned, "I need a couple of temperate souls on the team, and if they find my presence too intense and difficult to approach, they can safely let me know." A manager who knew she could be overpowering put it less delicately: "I have a couple of people on my staff who tell me when I'm full of crap." Another top executive, referring to our often used advice to "catch yourself," said, "I know I also need other people to 'catch' me."

On the most basic level, counterweights can be simple devices to help you avoid reflexively turning to a habitual behavior. One manager who couldn't seem to keep from monopolizing every conversation enlisted a peer and a direct report to signal him in meetings when he slipped into monologue mode.

Another overtalker actually "deputized" his assistant to interrupt him when he went off the rails, actually giving her a plastic sheriff's badge to flash at him.

On a more sophisticated level, counterweights by means of process or other people can help leaders correct their dysfunctional lopsided tendencies. William Lessor, for example, whose lopsidedness was predicated on the mindset that he was not smart enough, helped himself to be more strategic by putting in place a formal process for scanning the marketplace and working through the implications for the business. He also created a new position, chief of strategy, and filled the position with a gifted hire. Those moves helped to account for the quantum uptick in his effectiveness and confidence.

On an even grander scale, counterweights act as safety nets and reality checks for mercurially bold leaders who characteristically have trouble staying in bounds. In fact, the defining characteristic of breakthrough leaders is that they know no bounds—they envision the impossible and demand it of others. Steve Jobs, during his intense quest to invent and in short order commercialize the iPhone with its first-to-market touch screen and its irresistible design, had put in place a team capable of handling him, according to the biographer Walter Isaacson. "They all knew they were expected to be deferential to Jobs while also pushing back on his ideas and being willing to argue—a tricky balance to maintain." Tim Cook, the COO who after Job's death succeeded him, reported, "I realized very early on if you didn't voice your opinion he would mow you down." Cook had learned not to take Jobs' tantrums personally.

When we worked with Rich Spire, we realized that he was a leader who would get so focused on something he wanted to do that he would "steamroll over everybody" to get it done, regardless of the consequences. However, even he eventually learned to work with a loyal opposition, selecting individuals on his team who "for the most part felt comfortable challenging him." Still, the force of Spire's personality was such that his lieutenants discovered they had better luck raising issues in team meetings than going one-on-one with him. Strength in numbers.

For any leader, putting counterweights in place is important, but it is not enough. You then have to *allow* yourself to be influenced in the critical decisions you make and in the way you interact with people. You have to be able to tolerate the tension between what your instincts would have you do and where the counterweights might lead you. Sometimes, the tension can run screamingly high.

There is no better example of this in literature, or in life, than the passage in *Moby Dick* where Starbuck, the first mate, tells Ahab, the ship's captain, that they need to stop for repairs because precious whale oil is leaking out of the hold. Ahab, believing that they are in range of Moby Dick, the killer white whale, is not willing to interrupt his monomaniacal pursuit and he roughly orders Starbuck back up on deck. But Starbuck instead moves farther into the captain's cabin, his face reddening, and "with a daring" that is "strangely respectful" delicately presses his point. Ahab grabs a loaded musket and aims it at Starbuck. Still, Starbuck holds his ground and "mastering his emotion," says, "I ask thee not to beware of Starbuck; thou wouldst laugh; but let Ahab beware of Ahab; beware of thyself, old man." After Starbuck leaves, Ahab says to himself, "Ahab beware of Ahab—there is something there!" And he orders the crew to make the repairs.

By handling his boss with extraordinary skillfulness, a difficult-to-achieve blend of plain talk and deference, intensity and emotional control, Starbuck prevailed. His exchange with Ahab stands as a model for leaders who feel duty-bound to go up against their combustible, single-minded superiors, as well as for leaders who are unused to being challenged, but should be. Even Ahab, surely the most intransigent of superiors, sees the benefit—in this instance at least—of being confronted and influenced by a credible subordinate. Those who realize they cannot always check themselves had better learn to allow themselves to be kept in check by others.

Chapter 5

The Complete Leader

OF ALL THE LEADERS we have encountered, Will Stonecraft came closest to possessing ideal versatility. As the head of a major line of business in his company, Will was fluent both strategically and operationally and kept both perspectives in continual balance. He rarely talked strategy without considering the operational implications, and when he raised tactical issues, it was always in a strategic context. He had a singular ability, possessed by very few in- or outside of organizational life, to be absolutely, forcefully direct and at the same time nonthreatening. He was able to confront people with such tact that though they got the message loud and clear, they didn't so much feel confronted as considered, reassured, and improved. When he decided that an executive needed to be moved out of his or her role or from the company altogether, he did it in a good way that in most cases left the relationship intact. When it came to balancing yin and yang, he almost always got his settings right.

Although there is no such thing as a complete leader—in fact, only about 10 percent of the roughly 7,000 upper-level managers in our database even qualify as versatile—there are those rare individuals like Stonecraft who come very close. "I do not believe I have met anyone during my business career that compares to him," said one colleague. "He is a significant contributor to whatever challenge is presented to him; his vision, leadership, and motivational skills are exceptional. He leads without micromanaging. He teaches without being didactic. He's supremely capable without a bit of ego. He sets high expectations without browbeating anyone. He listens and understands without being passive. He empowers without overdelegating."

"I have seen him adeptly use every influence skill known to man," offered another coworker. "He can fluidly move from flattery, to alliance building, to quid pro quo negotiation, to admonishment, to employing rewards and recognition, and he can do this upward, downward, or sideways in the organization. He has all the tools in his arsenal, and he knows just when to use them. He pays attention to the signals, to what is really going on in the room. He is tuned in to 'the other.'"

Will Stonecraft's versatility is evident in his feedback report and, in particular, in his versatility wheel:

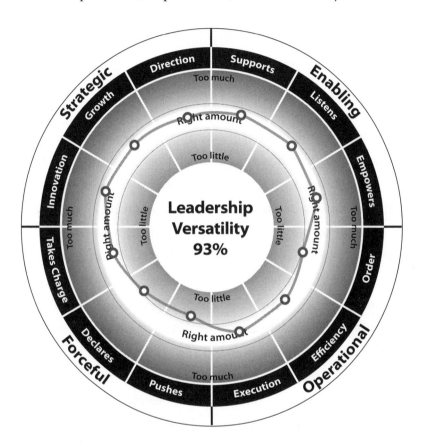

Stonecraft's profile is unusual in the degree to which his coworker ratings approximate a circle, hewing closely to the white band indicating "right amount." In fact, his 93 percent versatility rating indicates that his coworkers rated him "right amount" on the vast majority of the survey items. His profile is conspicuous for the absence of any prominent bulge or flat spot. The only two departures from optimal are his slightly too-little scores on "pushes" and "declares" (he has some trouble confronting direct reports about performance problems) and on "order" (he could be better organized personally).

In our experience with him, Stonecraft's rare versatility and finely tuned adaptability are founded upon one very basic, but very elusive, characteristic: a personal foundation sturdy enough to stand up to intense pressure though still flexible enough to bend but not break under pressure. Under adversity he experienced anxiety like any person would but he did not panic. He was able to think clearly and, as importantly, he steadied the senior people around him and, in his public appearances, served as a stabilizing influence for the entire organization.

Another way to characterize his personal foundation: he possessed an enviable blend of confidence and humility. He knew he was capable and yet fallible. He was secure in his knowledge of the industry and the business and yet entertained no illusions of omniscience. He could say, "I'm not sure what to do, give me your thoughts, let's think this through together" and not feel threatened or diminished. This hard-to-come-by combination of confidence and humility spelled inner versatility. Stonecraft was sure enough of himself that he could lead, but not so sure of himself that he couldn't learn. It was that mastery of internal opposites that made possible his mastery of leadership opposites.

Leaders who've mastered their internal opposites—the yin and yang of their own mindset—can be completely and passionately engaged and at the same time utterly calm. This precious state is sometimes called "relaxed concentration." Psychologist Mihaly Csikszentmihalyi has famously referred to it as "flow," a condition in which "attention can be freely invested to achieve a person's goals, because there is no disorder to straighten out, no threat to the self to defend against." It is freedom from excessive self-concern, freedom from clamoring ego needs. Will Stonecraft was credited with this mental freedom by a colleague who said, "He is tuned into what people are doing and what is really going on in the room. He's not thinking, 'What are other people thinking about me?'"

It is this mental state that makes for optimal performance in any capacity. It is what enables athletes to play "heads-up" ball, point guards to have court vision, quarterbacks under pressure to find an open receiver, and great race-car drivers to attain high speeds and brake at the last millisecond. Flow is the state of mind that allows them to quickly and incisively yet calmly read a game situation and apply their skills in the right combination, at the right time, and with the right "touch."

The Route to Versatility

To become a more nearly complete leader, we believe you need to do three things: accept yourself, test yourself, and offset yourself.

Accept Yourself

To grow and improve, it isn't enough to know yourself. You must unflinchingly reconcile yourself to the reality of who you are and how you lead. Like it or not, this is what is not effective about your way of leading. Proud of it or not, this is what makes you tick. Ultimately, to accept yourself is to look at yourself as if you are somebody else.

Consider the head of a successful nonprofit agency who micromanaged to the nth degree, to the detriment of his organization and his own health. It became clear to us in conversation with him that his behavior was driven by a fear of getting fired, but he could not admit that to himself. "Anxiety is a sign of weakness," he told us. As the poet Dylan Thomas once said, we live in fear of fear. Once the executive was able to acknowledge that he was afraid, he was better equipped to change his mindset and behavior. His twin goal read as follows: "Control my anxiety, not every detail." Surveyed several months later, his staff noted change for the better. With his anxiety under better control his self-confidence had increased. "I am a lot more comfortable in my own skin." In effect, he had firmed up his personal foundation.

Although that was an archetypal case of learning to catch oneself, to consciously dial back behavior by reining in its underlying compulsion, subconscious fears can lead to inhibitions. Therefore, *dialing up* certain behaviors is an equally important part of becoming a complete leader. One top executive who well knew he should manage by walking around and, in fact, had a real talent for it nevertheless remained curiously office-bound. It turned out that he assumed that people would be offended if he didn't know their names or wasn't aware of what they were working on. The underlying fear was of rejection. As we explored the inhibition he made the connection to his childhood: he had often been odd man out in his neighborhood. "I realize now," he said, "that people will give me more slack than I think." It was no picnic for him to own up to his twisted logic and the underlying dread, but once freed from his fearful assumption, he dialed up that small but significant part of his role.

Dialing back and dialing up are two sides of the same coin. When you are no longer investing too much in one side of leadership, you are free to invest more in the other side. But don't count on having the underused behavior dial itself up naturally. Both overuse and underuse have to be actively addressed.

Self-acceptance doesn't exclusively entail admitting our faults and our hang-ups. It can also entail internalizing what others appreciate about us. Rick Freed, a senior manager, got great grades in his feedback report, but could not accept the praise. "The positives are overwhelming to me," he said. In conversation it emerged that he had spent a lifetime being afraid that he didn't "measure up." Eventually, he convinced himself that indeed he didn't and no amount of positive feedback could counter that belief. To accept praise, he had to first accept his fear. To accept yourself is to be courageously objective about yourself, inside and out. When Rick was finally able to do that, he said, "The realization is very liberating." An apt choice of words. It liberated him to be more vocal and influential in senior forums. "I realized that I had a voice that could be effective in shaping the corporation's strategy," he said. "I'm much more open, confident, willing to speak my mind." Firming up his shaky foundation made all the difference: "I'm not always walking on that tightrope, feeling that if I make a misstep I'll fall off."

Test Yourself

The accumulation of new experience, whether you choose it or it chooses you, is a ticket to growing and improving. It is by repeatedly testing yourself, by taking the attitude that you will do your best to rise to every important occasion, however big, that you outgrow the unfortunate legacies of childhood and grow as a leader and as a person. At the neurological level, this continual process takes advantage of the plasticity of the brain and literally rewires it.

We come into this world equipped with 100 billion brain cells—as many as there are stars in the Milky Way—ready to be fired up. It is the alchemy of experience that turns this malleable universe of potential into a unique human intellect, personality, and memory. From the day we are born, everything we see, hear, feel, touch, taste, or smell fires a tiny spark that solders a distinct neural connection. In a very real sense, we become the sum of all our experiences. This electrical storm, however, is not confined to the early years of life as was once thought. It is now accepted that the human brain continues to regenerate over the course of a lifetime. As long as we live, our synaptic patterns continue to adapt to new experiences in an organizational ebb and flow that is constantly re-creating who we are.

The stimulus of new experience outside your comfort zone can slowly but surely redefine and shore up the structure of your self. Neurons grow and branch and make ever more subtle connections, making us better able to deal with paradox and complexity, more likely to keep a level head in a crisis and be a calming influence on others. It can take years of fresh experience to have an effect on the primitive part of the brain where sensitivities and pain are lodged, but just as a coral reef grows bit by organismic bit, even managers with chronic feelings of inadequacy can build up their faith in themselves.

Albert Ellis, a pioneering thinker on how to break out of dysfunctional patterns, tells how as a young adult he was painfully shy with women. To fight his shyness, over the course of three months he attempted to strike up a conversation with 130 different women he didn't know. In the majority of cases he got a good response. After that, although talking to women still wasn't easy for him, it was possible. Doing something repeatedly that you had been avoiding is known as desensitization, a proven technique for getting over a phobia. The idea is to string together a series of small wins that demonstrate you can do something and that doing it will produce good results. It is a form of dialing up an underused behavior—*forcing* yourself rather than *catching* yourself, if you will.

Another way to force yourself is to create a structure or process that necessitates the unused or underused behavior. A manager who had a hard time holding people accountable received this advice from a colleague: "Look, you and I are not table pounders. The only way we're going to be as tough as we need to be is to set up mechanisms that require us to be that way." To act on the advice, the manager also had to get over "a long-time aversion to any kind of bureaucratic structures." Heeding the advice, the manager instituted regular operating reviews. "Now we meet twice a month to make sure the basics happen." What he learned is that structure is an enabler. There is no end to how inventive and resourceful you can be in devising mechanisms that leave you no choice but to act in a new way.

This applies equally to leaders who overdo it. Workaholics, for example, who simply can't stop themselves, even at the risk of their relationships and their own well-being, can benefit from rigid structure. It often helps them to create a figurative wall that surrounds and protects their personal or family time. In the mind of the workaholic, this wall has to be made of thick, steel-reinforced concrete, an ironclad commitment to the others in his life buttressed by making his coworkers aware that the wall is inviolable. This is a huge desensitization challenge. At first, he finds it uncomfortable, even impossible, to stop thinking about work in his down time. But the rigidity of the structure will eventually win out and his personal foundation will strengthen.

Sometimes we test ourselves and at other times we are tested by circumstance. When the stimulus of new experience and the need to grow is thrust upon us, it's a test we can pass only if we view it from the right perspective. Problems aren't problems; they are opportunities to be capable. Adversity is a great teacher, whether it comes from within or without. The measure of the success of the test is the discomfort, the *stretching*, it causes. As William James advised: "Do, every day or two, something for no other reason than you would rather not do it, so that when the hour of dire need draws nigh, it might find you not unnerved and untrained to stand the test."

Offset Yourself

There is great good in working on yourself. In addition to the practical benefits, it's a way of retaining your youthful energy. The moment you stop growing is the moment you grow old. Yet as much as you shore up your weaknesses, you will never be strong in all important areas. As much as you learn to curb your excesses, you will remain at risk, however attenuated, of overplaying your strengths. To seek literal perfection in yourself is a fool's errand. Fortunately, being effective in your role doesn't have to all come from you. Indeed, it *can't* all come from you.

One way to offset yourself is, as we saw in the previous chapter, is to employ counterweights. In his 1830s book on democracy in America, Alexis de Tocqueville wrote: "In absolute monarchies the ruinous principle is the unlimited and unreasonable extension of royal power. Any measure that takes away the counter-weights left by the constitution to balance this power is radically bad, even though the effects may long seem negligible." To leaders not vested with anything remotely like royal power, the same warning applies. You must put counterbalancing people and processes in place and then allow them to influence you, even when it hurts, all the while being neither too resistant to those influences nor too receptive to them.

Steve Jobs, a leader of prodigious intellect and undeniable personal power, was temperamental and overpowering to the end, yet he was capable of backing down. At a key juncture in the design of a breakout product, one of his direct reports took a strong, emotional stand against the chip maker Jobs planned to use. Jobs relented, saying simply, "I can't go against my best guys."

The other way to offset yourself is to do what leaders everywhere know to do—compensate for your weaknesses. The one thing we will add to this conventional wisdom is that you must avoid the trap of disparaging the side of leadership that is the opposite of what you are good at. A newly appointed CEO whose forte was running operations fell into the trap. Asked what it would mean to pay more attention to strategy, he said, "I'll have to spend more fluff time." To compensate for your weaknesses, you must value what you lack.

Central to offsetting yourself in either way is to stock your team and organization with high-quality people, never settling for less. A secret to Steve Jobs' success is he insisted on having the best people in key roles. In this spirit, Sandy Ogg stated that "the difference between a good CEO and a great one is the ability to attract big people."

You can, then, approximate complete leadership by accepting, testing, and offsetting yourself—and continually growing in your capacity to do each of those things. In concert with the right array of talent, you can function like a wheel that is close to truly round and therefore equipped to travel smoothly over rugged roads.

Notes

Introduction

Buckingham, Marcus, and Donald Clifton. (2001). *Now, Discover Your Strengths*. New York: Simon & Schuster.

"Analyses of derailed . . ." McCall, M. W., and M. M. Lombardo (1983). *Off the Track: Why and How Successful Executives Get Derailed* (Report #21). Greensboro, NC: Center for Creative Leadership.

Chapter 1

Anderson, Sherwood. (1919). *Winesburg, Ohio: A Group of Tales of Ohio Small-Town Life*. New York: B. W. Heubsch.

Aristotle, c. 325 B.C. *Nicomachean Ethics* (English), II.1109a27, p. 111.

McLean, Bethany. (2004). *The Smartest Guys in the Room: The Amazing Rise and Scandalous Fall of Enron*. New York: Portfolio.

"In one study . . ." Gallup StrengthsFinder instrument. Rath, Tom. (February 2007). *StrengthsFinder 2.0*. Gallup

Press. Study linking the StrengthsFinder themes to overdoing associated leader behavior, underdoing complementary behaviors: Kaiser, R. B., and D. V. Overfield. (2011). "Strengths, strengths overused, and lopsided leadership," *Consulting Psychology Journal: Practice and Research, 63*, 89–109.

Chapter 2

"In the course . . ." The Forceful-Enabling, Strategic-Operational model of leadership comes from three sources. First, these are the concepts and terms our executive clients use to describe one another's performance. Second, the academic study of leadership over the last 100 years has used analogous concepts. And finally, statistical analyses of our measure, the *Leadership Versatility Index*, have produced these four distinct factors. For details, see the appendix in: Kaplan, R., and Robert Kaiser. (2006). *The Versatile Leader: Make the Most of Your Strengths—Without Overdoing It*. San Francisco: Pfeiffer; and R. B. Kaiser, and D. V. Overfield. (2010). "Assessing flexible leadership as a mastery of opposites," *Consulting Psychology Journal: Practice and Research, 62*, 105–118.

"The dynamic tension . . ." Kaiser, R. B., J. L. McGinnis, and D. V. Overfield. (2012). "The how and the what of leadership," *Consulting Psychology Journal: Practice and Research, 64*, 119–135.

"The inverse relationship . . ." Regarding the inverse correlations between forceful and enabling leadership and between strategic and operational leadership: In the normative database for the current LVI (version 3.1) with ratings for over 5,000 upper-level managers, the correlation between opposing behaviors is –.72 for

Forceful-Enabling and –.30 for Strategic-Operational. (The weaker correlation for Strategic-Operational is due to a relatively low incidence of "too much" ratings on Strategic.) These negative correlations provide robust evidence for the "polarity effect"—the tendency for managers to overemphasize one side to the neglect of the other side in a pair of complementary behaviors.

"In another study . . ." Kaiser, R. B. and R. E. Kaplan. (2009). When strengths run amok (pp. 57-76). In Robert B. Kaiser (Ed.) The Perils of Accentuating the Positive. Tulsa, OK: Hogan Press. Douglas McGregor. (2006). *The Human Side of Enterprise.* New York: McGraw-Hill.

Zaleznik, Abraham. (1989). *The Managerial Mystique: Restoring Leadership in Business.* New York: Harper & Row.

"Jerry Hunt, former . . ." Hunt, J. G. (1991). *Leadership: A New Synthesis.* Newbury Park, CA: Sage.

"One of many studies . . ." Janovics, J. E., and N. D. Christiansen. (2003). "Profiling new business development: Personality correlates of ideation and implementation," *Social Behavior and Personality, 31,* 71–80.

"In a recent study . . ." Kaiser, R. B., and J. Hogan. (2011). "Personality, leader behavior, and overdoing it," *Consulting Psychology Journal: Practice and Research, 63,* 219–242.

"The saga of Steve . . ." Isaacson, W. (2011). *Steve Jobs.* New York: Simon & Schuster, p. 569.

". . . an exceptionally strong association . . ." Kaiser, R. B., D. V. Overfield, and R. E. Kaplan. (2010). *Leadership Versatility Index version 3.0 Facilitator's Guide.* Greensboro, NC: Kaplan DeVries, Inc.

Chapter 3

"Among professional athletes . . ." Loehr, James E. (1986). *Mental Toughness Training for Sports: Achieving Athletic Excellence.* Brattleboro, VT: Stephen Greene Press.

"As Napoleon summed it up. . ." Emerson, R. W. (1968). "Napoleon: Man of the World." From *Selected writings of Ralph Waldo Emerson.* Atkinson, B. (Ed.). New York: Modern Library.

Chapter 4

Leadership Versatility Index. Issued to Robert E. Kaplan and Robert B. Kaiser of Kaplan DeVries Inc. on October 17, 2006, as U.S. Patent No. 7,121,830: Method for Collecting, Analyzing, and Reporting Data on Skills and Personal Attributes. Instrument now published and distributed by Kaiser Leadership Solutions, www.kaiserleadership.com. The LVI's scale is:

". . . in a Malcolm Gladwell 'blink.'" Gladwell, Malcolm. (2007). *Blink: The Power of Thinking Without Thinking.* New York: Back Bay Books.

Carnegie, Dale. (1975). *How to Stop Worrying and Start Living.* New York: Simon & Schuster.

Loehr, Jim, and Tony Schwartz. (January 2001). "The Making of a Corporate Athlete," *Harvard Business Review,* R0101H.

"William James, who . . ." James, William. (1890). *Principles of Psychology,* pp. 136, 149.

"[Koufax] was able . . ." Leavy, Jane. (2002). *Sandy Koufax: A Lefty's Legacy.* New York: HarperCollins.

"Psychoanalytic thinker, Karen Horney . . ." Horney, Karen. (1950). *Neurosis and Human Growth.* New York: Norton.

"Andre Agassi the eight-time . . ." Agassi, Andre. (2010). *Open.* New York: Vintage Books.

". . . devised by developmental psychologist Robert Kegan at Harvard." Kegan, Robert, and Lisa Laskow. (2009). From *Immunity to Change: How to Overcome It and Unlock the Potential in Yourself and Your Organization (Leadership for the Common Good)*. Boston: Harvard Business School Press.

"As Peter Drucker said . . ." From the dust jacket of Buckingham, Marcus, and Donald Clifton. (2001). *Now, Discover Your Strengths.* New York: Simon & Schuster.

Melville, Herman. (1851). *Moby-Dick,* or *The Whale.*

Chapter 5

"This precious state . . ." Csikszentmihalyi, Mihaly. (1990). *Flow: The Psychology of Optimal Experience.* New York: HarperCollins.

"At the neurological level, . . ." Pascual-Leone, A., A. Amedi, F. Fregni, and L. B. Merabet. (2005). "The plastic human brain cortex," *Annual Review of Neuroscience,* 28, 377–401. See also, Chaney, Warren (2007). *Dynamic Mind.* Las Vegas: Houghton-Brace Publishing.

"Albert Ellis, a pioneering . . ." Ellis, Albert, and Russel Grieger, with contributors. (1977). *Handbook of Rational-Emotive Therapy.* New York: Springer Publishing.

"As William James advised . . ." James, Williams. (1980). From *The Selected Letters of William James.* Hardwick, E. (Ed.). Boston: D. R. Godine.

"... desensitization, a proven technique for getting over a phobia." Joseph Wolpe, and Arnold Lazarus. (1996). *Behavior Therapy Techniques.* Oxford: Pergamon Press.

Tocqueville, Alexis de. (2000). *Democracy in America.* Translated, edited, and with an introduction by Harvey C. Mansfield and Delba Winthrop. Chicago: University of Chicago Press. "Jobs relented, saying . . ." Isaacson, Walter. (2011). *Steve Jobs,* p. 492. New York: Simon & Schuster.

"Sandy Ogg stated . . ." *Book of Wisdom.* Blackstone, internal publication, 2012.

Acknowledgments

We are immensely grateful to our editor, Chris Bergonzi, whose perfect pitch was indispensable to our effort to make the book clear, cogent, and readable.

We are also grateful to Court Carruthers, Mike Cole, Jeff DeLapp, David DeVries, Gerry Fine, Darren Overfield, Sally Savoia, and Dean Stamoulis for critiquing the first draft and, in Jeff's and Court's case, the rewritten manuscript.

Special thanks to Donald Kaplan, Bob's brother, who in long, nuanced conversations illuminated the reader's experience, taking to heart our goal of making that experience a good one.

Index

stupid, fear of being, 68
"swing thought," 62–63

talents, undermining of, 9
talking too much, 14
team, influence of, 9
technical functions, vs. general
    management, 47–48
tendencies, reform of, 65
tension, tolerating, 79
test yourself, 88–92
Theory X (McGregor), 24
Theory Y (McGregor), 24
therapy, vs. developmental work,
    5
Thomas, Dylan, 86
360-degree evaluation
    LVI example of, 60
    managers' ratings in, 2
    seminal moment in, 1–2
Tocqueville, Alexis de, 92–93
trust, of self, 66
truth
    becoming falsehood, 10
    in leading, 38
"tyranny of the shoulds," 70–71

underestimation, of self, 73

"versatile leadership," 38
versatility, route to. *See also* lead-
    ership versatility
    accept yourself, 86–88
    offset yourself, 92–94
    test yourself, 88–92
"versatility wheel," 51–52, 83. *See
    also* Leadership Versatility
    Index (LVI)
vision, articulation of, 7–8
vocal power, 44–45

weakness/weaknesses
    compensating for, 93
    extreme use of talents as, 9
    leadership development and, 2
    overused strengths as, 10, 15
Weeks, Wendell, 35
Winesburg, Ohio (Anderson), 10
workaholics, 91
worldview, 37
worth, proving, 66

yin-yang concept/symbol, 17, 34

Zaleznik, Abraham, 24–25

About the Authors

BOB KAPLAN is president of
Kaplan DeVries Inc, specialists in
assessing leaders for selection and for
development. With Wilfred Drath
and Joan Kofodimos, Bob introduced
a forerunner of executive coaching.
With them he published Beyond *Ambition: How Driven
Managers Can Lead Better and Live Better.* He built an
early 360 survey (SKILLscope for Managers), and he
came up with the idea for a different breed of 360, the
patented Leadership Versatility Index, which he and
Rob Kaiser developed and commercialized.

An honorary senior fellow at the Center for Creative Leadership, he has a B.A. and Ph.D. from Yale
University. He lives in New York City with his wife
Becky.

You can reach him at bobkaplan@kaplandevries.
com or log onto http://kaplandevries.com

ROB KAISER is nuts about the subject of leadership. He consults to leaders and their teams, conducts original research, and creates innovative tools for assessment and development. Rob is the author, co-author, and editor of  five books, and a highly regarded public speaker who presents his engaging and provocative views to professional audiences around the world. He and Bob Kaplan were awarded a patent for the revolutionary features in their next-generation assessment instrument, the Leadership Versatility Index.

Rob's research and development work is based on a blend of behavioral science and extensive consulting work that ranges from coaching high potentials to helping CEOs articulate their expectations for senior leaders and using that blueprint to transform the leadership culture.

Rob began his career at the Center for Creative Leadership and joined the executive development firm, Kaplan DeVries Inc., in 1997. He was named partner in 2005. In 2012, he formed Kaiser Leadership Solutions to create and tools for assessment and development that set a new standard for innovation and impact.

Rob received an M.S. in Organizational Psychology from Illinois State University; the College of Arts and Sciences named him alumnus of the year in 2007.

You can reach him at rob@kaiserleadership.com

About CCL

THE CENTER FOR CREATIVE LEADERSHIP (CCL) is a top-ranked global provider of executive education that unlocks individual and organizational potential through its exclusive focus on leadership education and research. The *Financial Times* has ranked CCL's public programs in the top ten internationally for ten consecutive years. Founded in 1970 as a nonprofit educational institution, CCL helps clients worldwide cultivate creative leadership—the capacity to achieve more than imagined by thinking and acting beyond boundaries— through an array of programs, products, and other services. CL is headquartered in Greensboro, North Carolina, with campuses in Colorado Springs, Colorado; San Diego, California; Brussels, Belgium; and Singapore; and with offices in Pune, India and in Moscow. Supported by more than four hundred faculty members and staff, it works annually with more than twenty thousand leaders and two thousand organizations. In addition, twelve Network Associates around the world offer selected CCL programs and assessments.

Berrett–Koehler
Publishers

Berrett-Koehler is an independent publisher dedicated to an ambitious mission: *Creating a World That Works for All.*

We believe that to truly create a better world, action is needed at all levels—individual, organizational, and societal. At the individual level, our publications help people align their lives with their values and with their aspirations for a better world. At the organizational level, our publications promote progressive leadership and management practices, socially responsible approaches to business, and humane and effective organizations. At the societal level, our publications advance social and economic justice, shared prosperity, sustainability, and new solutions to national and global issues.

A major theme of our publications is "Opening Up New Space." Berrett-Koehler titles challenge conventional thinking, introduce new ideas, and foster positive change. Their common quest is changing the underlying beliefs, mindsets, institutions, and structures that keep generating the same cycles of problems, no matter who our leaders are or what improvement programs we adopt.

We strive to practice what we preach—to operate our publishing company in line with the ideas in our books. At the core of our approach is stewardship, which we define as a deep sense of responsibility to administer the company for the benefit of all of our "stakeholder" groups: authors, customers, employees, investors, service providers, and the communities and environment around us.

We are grateful to the thousands of readers, authors, and other friends of the company who consider themselves to be part of the "BK Community." We hope that you, too, will join us in our mission.

A BK Business Book

This book is part of our BK Business series. BK Business titles pioneer new and progressive leadership and management practices in all types of public, private, and nonprofit organizations. They promote socially responsible approaches to business, innovative organizational change methods, and more humane and effective organizations.

Berrett–Koehler
Publishers

A community dedicated to creating
a world that works for all

Visit Our Website: www.bkconnection.com

Read book excerpts, see author videos and Internet movies, read
our authors' blogs, join discussion groups, download book apps, find
out about the BK Affiliate Network, browse subject-area libraries of
books, get special discounts, and more!

Subscribe to Our Free E-Newsletter, the *BK Communiqué*

Be the first to hear about new publications, special discount offers,
exclusive articles, news about bestsellers, and more! Get on the list
for our free e-newsletter by going to **www.bkconnection.com**.

Get Quantity Discounts

Berrett-Koehler books are available at quantity discounts for orders
of ten or more copies. Please call us toll-free at (800) 929-2929 or
email us at bkp.orders@aidcvt.com.

Join the BK Community

BKcommunity.com is a virtual meeting place where people from
around the world can engage with kindred spirits to create a world
that works for all. **BKcommunity.com** members may create their own
profiles, blog, start and participate in forums and discussion groups,
post photos and videos, answer surveys, announce and register for
upcoming events, and chat with others online in real time. Please join
the conversation!

Certified

Corporation
bcorporation.net